$4.00
B(0 +
2.18

D0710099

Marita Golden

Migrations
of the Heart

Marita Golden has written both fiction and nonfiction, including *Don't Play in the Sun*, *A Miracle Every Day*, and *Saving Our Sons*. She is the editor of *Wild Women Don't Wear No Blues: Black Women Writers on Love, Men, and Sex*, and the coeditor of *Gumbo: An Anthology of African American Writing*. She is the founder and CEO of the Hurston/Wright Foundation, which supports African American writers, and lives in Maryland.

Also by Marita Golden

A Woman's Place

Long Distance Life

Wild Women Don't Wear No Blues:
Black Women Writers on Love, Men and Sex (editor)

And Do Remember Me

Saving Our Sons: Raising Black Children in a Turbulent World

Skin Deep: Black Women and White Women Write About Race
(editor, with Susan Richards Shreve)

A Miracle Every Day: Triumph and Transformation
in the Lives of Single Mothers

The Edge of Heaven

Gumbo: A Celebration of African American Writing
(editor, with E. Lynn Harris)

Don't Play in the Sun:
One Woman's Journey Through the Color Complex

Migrations
of the Heart

An Autobiography

Marita Golden

Anchor Books
A Division of Random House, Inc.
NEW YORK

ANCHOR BOOKS TRADE PAPERBACK EDITION, JANUARY 2005

Copyright © 1983 by Marita Golden

All rights reserved under International and Pan-American Copyright
Conventions. Published in the United States by Anchor Books, a division of Random House, Inc., New York, and simultaneously in Canada
by Random House of Canada Limited, Toronto. Originally published in
hardcover by Anchor Books, Garden City, New York, in 1983.

Anchor Books and colophon are registered trademarks
of Random House, Inc.

The Library of Congress has cataloged the previous Anchor Books
hardcover edition as follows:
Golden, Marita.
Migrations of the heart.
1. Golden, Marita. 2. Afro-Americans—Washington, D.C.—Autobiography. 3. Washington (D.C.)—Autobiography. 4. Afro-Americans—
Nigeria—Autobiography. 5. Nigeria—Social life and customs. I. Title.
F205.N4G64 1983 305.8'96073'024 [B]
82-45248

Anchor ISBN: 1-4000-7831-8

www.anchorbooks.com

Printed in the United States of America
10 9 8 7 6

To my father, who told me the stories that matter.
To my mother, who taught me to remember them.

I wish to thank:

Marie Dutton Brown, for always believing

Sidney Offit, for helping ME to believe

Louise Fleming—she knows why

Lorraine Broy—she does too

Laura Van Wormer, for the enthusiasm she brought to this project

Carol Mann, for seeing a story worth telling where I saw only a life

1. *Beginnings*

1

My father was the first man I ever loved. He was as assured as a panther. His ebony skin was soft as the surface of coal. The vigorous scent of El Producto cigars was a perfume that clung to him. The worn leather seat of his taxi, a stubborn aroma, had seeped into his pores, and like a baptism the smells rubbed onto me from the palms of his hands.

In school he went as far as the sixth grade, then learned the rest on his own. Part of the rest he bequeathed to me—gold nuggets of fact, myth, legend dropped in the lap of my mind, shiny new pennies meant to be saved. By his own definition he was "a black man and proud of it." Arming me with a measure of this conviction, he unfolded a richly colored tapestry, savored its silken texture and warned me never to forget its worth.

Africa: "It wasn't dark until the white man got there."

Cleopatra: "I don't care WHAT they tell you in school, she was a black woman."

Hannibal: "He crossed the Alps with an army of five hundred elephants."

The Sphinx (pointing with a tobacco-stained index finger to a page in the encyclopedia): "Look at the nose, see how broad it is? That's your nose. That's my nose too."

Bitter, frightening tales of slavery dredged by his great-grandparents from memories that refused to be mute. Passed to him. Passed to me. And when he recounted the exploits of Toussaint L'Ouverture, pausing to remind me that L'Ouverture meant "The Opener," inside his eyes I saw fire and smoke float over the hills of Haiti, and his voice stalked the room amid the clanging of swords, the stomp of heavy boots.

Our most comfortable stage was his taxicab. On frigid winter Saturday afternoons and warm summer evenings, I rode in the front seat with him. Always, it was an adventure. As much as anything else in his life, my father cherished the look of surprise and unease that invaded the faces of white passengers as he regaled them with quotes from Jefferson, Tolstoy or Frederick Douglass. Pouncing on them unawares with the sharpness of his intellect, he brought their blanched faces from behind *The Wall Street Journal* or the New York *Times*. Their baffled respect, blooming in the form of a generous tip or an awed, "Mister, you're pretty smart," sealed his victory.

Together we visited the homes of women, who plied me with Kool-Aid and cookies and spoke to him in a language of double meanings and invisible but obvious desire. Women adored my father. He took them seriously enough to strip his fantasies before them. He listened as intensely as he spoke, and his reactions confirmed the legitimacy of their dreams. All of his women were like my mother, women who had turned daydream desire into tangible reality through houses, cars, money. All theirs. And, like my mother, these women, who had flexed their muscles in the face of fate and circumstance, looked at him with eyes that said, "I will give this all to you." My father never refused anything. He accepted their allegiance or a loan of money with equal ease as his due. He was a hard, nearly impossible man to love when love meant exclusive rights to his soul. Yet he relied on their steadfastness to enhance the improvisational nature of his life. Hearing their screen doors slam behind us as we walked to my father's cab, I trembled as though implicated in a crime. For, returning home, I met my mother's worried interrogation and watched her large hands tie themselves in knots after I helplessly nodded in assent when she asked if we'd visited Dorothy or Mamie that day.

My father's friends were men with names like Lucky and Sweets, men whose eyes rendered other verdicts on their lives. I watched them develop potbellies and saw gray sprout at their hairlines as they stood, year after year, before the fire-engine-red Coke machine in Sam's Sunoco gas station, waiting for the number to come out. In a shifting, eternal circle, they parried and joked, voices edgy, cloaked in gruff humor as they stood wondering if 301 or 513 would come out that day and "make them a man." Because of his luck with women and money, they called my father Goldie.

They were not his real friends—they feared him too much. Shuddered in the wake of his determination, which cast consideration aside. And they trembled, windswept and lost, in the face of his poorly hidden belief that he was and always would be better than the rest. Much like the characters who peopled the Africa he created for me, and for whom he felt an unbridled affinity, my father viewed his life as a stage. Those around him were an audience from whom he demanded total loyalty but to whom he gave mere lightning flashes of his soul. And I loved him with blind faith. Could never imagine having to forgive him anything. So when I had to, I could not.

My father grabbed life by the arm and wrestled it into squealing submission. My mother cleared the same terrain with a faith and self-possession that both fueled and ruined some of her dreams.

Greensboro, North Carolina, must have fit her like a coat too small, buttons missing, hem unraveling and torn. The town, steeped and cured in humility and patience, could never have imagined her hopes. So at nineteen she fled. One summer night, while her parents and younger brothers slept, she crept out of bed. Crouching on the floor, she retrieved a cardboard suitcase wrapped in string that had been hidden beneath her bed for three days. After pinning a note to her pillow, she walked out into the full-moon night. Standing on the porch, she felt her heart hacking a path out of her chest. Placing the suitcase on the porch, she rubbed her sweating palms on the side of her dress. Crickets echoed in the night air and fireflies illuminated the web of knee-high front-yard grass. And, as on every evening of what had been her life up to then, the pure, heartfelt country silence reached out for her. Struggling out of its grasp, she picked up the suitcase. Licked her lips for courage. And, imagining her mother's face the next morning discovering the empty bed and her wizened hands reaching for the letter, she scurried down the steps. It was 1928 and she was headed north.

Washington, D.C., was as far north as she got. There she settled with a cousin who'd arrived the year before. Her first job was cleaning government office buildings. But soon she discovered more gratifying outlets for her industry. Driven by caution, she scrupulously saved her earnings yet daringly, shrewdly bet small amounts on the numbers. She hit them regularly and plowed the winnings into property. Soon she owned four boarding houses and leased two others, a material affluence which at that time equaled a virtual empire for a black woman. Indeed, my mother was blessed, for she had her own. Each month, when she wrote her parents, she slipped a money order between the pages of the folded letter. And seven years after her arrival in the city dotted with historical monuments and scarred by Jim Crow laws, my mother drove, prosperous and proud, back to Greensboro in her own 1935 Ford.

Her mother sat on the porch in a rocking chair, stringing beans that afternoon. Her feet touched the splintered boards and she set the bowl of beans on the table beside her, stood up and clutched the banister. "Be-A-trice, whose car that you drivin?" she called out with only modest interest.

"It's mine, mama," her daughter called back, parking the car before the house with considerable skill.

"Yours?"

"Yes, mama, mine."

My mother was now walking dramatically up the steps to the porch. She wore a dark-purple suit and a hat that resembled a box was perched on her head. Her hands held white gloves and a small brown leather clutch bag.

"You want to go for a ride?" she asked, delighted to be offering such a treat.

Her mother, who had witnessed greater miracles than this every Sunday in church, merely folded her arms and shook her head in disgruntled amazement. "Be-A-trice, can't you write your own folks no more? It's been three months since we last heard from you."

If she'd had her way, my mother would have been an actress. Like the best of them, her presence was irresistible. My father used words to control and keep others at bay. For my mother language was a way to reassure and reward. My father demanded loyalty. My mother inspired it in the host of friends whom she cared for and melded into her life. She was a large, buxom woman, with caramel-colored skin and a serene face that gave little indication of the passion with which she imbued every wish, every commitment. Her hands were large, long-fingered. Serious hands that rendered punishment swiftly and breathlessly, folded sheets and dusted tables in a succession of white folks' homes long after she was mistress of several of her own. Hands that offered unconditional shelter and love. In every picture of her there is freeze-framed a look of sadness rippling across her glance, as though there is still just one more thing she wants to own, to do, to know. She wore perfume, fox fur throws casually slung over her shoulders and lamb coats, as though born to wear nothing less. My father confided to me offhandedly once, "When I met your mother I thought she was the most beautiful woman I'd ever seen."

She had been married once before. That husband had loved her with a precision and concern my father could never imagine. But after ten years she divorced him, his spirit routed, mauled by years of drinking into a shape she could barely recognize.

My father was her Armageddon. The thirteen years of their marriage, a music box wound too tight, played an off-key song of separation and reunion. The arguments and fights were nearly always murderous. Sculpted like hot wax around the dry bones of their unyielding wills was a love that joined and informed them of each other in ways that were unbearable and soothing. They fought over my father's women. But mostly, with a special viciousness, over power, symbolized by my mother's property. Her will shimmered with so much eloquence and strength that my father felt duty bound to try to break it. He almost did.

Year after year he insisted the houses be put in his name. Some were, and my father lost them with obscene swiftness, bartering them to pay his own gambling debts. My mother, now more reckless than wise and entrapped and enshrined by her love for my father, lost the rest. She gambled the way she had lived her life—with everything she had. Soon the modest empire dwindled to one house. Like pearls falling to the floor, the houses scattered, rolling across my mother's hopes into unseen cracks and crevices. Finally, irretrievable.

In the wake of a fight, my father, a wounded lion, would storm out of the house. A chaste calm settled over us all then. A peace so unfamiliar, so welcome that my mother was rarely comfortable with it. Perhaps within it she heard the mocking voice of a solitude she could neither accept nor respect. Maybe she missed the purpose, the scratching, blood-pumping tension my father provided. I think she was afraid. But my father always returned, swaggering, triumphant, forgiven. Pounced on at the front door by me with kisses, arms, legs enfolding. Greeted by my mother with a faint resigned smile that resembled relief.

Still, my mother suffered inside the silence of that marriage. A silence that was loudest during the fight, the argument, the shout. During the last, most bitter years of their union she frequently sought renewal through pilgrimages to the home of her former husband. Some evenings I went with her to his small basement apartment. We ate dinner around a card table in the center of the disheveled but clean room. As a centerpiece, a plastic flower sat in an empty coffee jar. As my mother talked, Mr. Robinson listened gratefully, his gray eyes shining in the dim half-light. The room was stuffed with tightly packed cardboard boxes that sat beneath year-old funeral home calendars tacked to the wall. Sometimes I napped on an iron folding cot in a corner.

Drifting between sleep and wakefulness, I heard their voices waltz overhead, hushed but not hiding. My father's women handed him the tools with which to conquer them. Mr. Robinson gave my mother a way to stay alive.

But it was the houses that really mattered. And years after the fact, my mother was never able to understand or forgive herself for losing them. Sunday afternoons she used to pack me, one of her girl friends, and the woman's daughter into her 1958 Pontiac and drive around Washington looking at houses. She sat behind the steering wheel and discussed them with Miss Johnnie Mae as though she was choosing a dress for a special occasion.

In the houses we lived in she paid homage to the home she'd known in Greensboro. For she crowded the mantelpieces and shelves with the same abundance of tiny ceramic knickknacks, doilies and plants, cherished only for Sunday china, that her mother had used to bring grace to the tiny house on McConnell Road. And, as at my grandmother's house, all the houses had large back yards and screened-in back porches. She would put cast-off sofas there in the summer and gossip with the people next door while stirring a pitcher of iced tea. The houses were solid, unequivocal. Proper Victorian houses that demanded a certain majesty of their owners. On Saturday mornings we attacked the house in a frenzy of cleaning. While my mother polished the hardwood floors, I swept down three flights of stairs and hallways that never ended. Dusted the dark-brown massive bureaus in her bedroom, the upright piano, and vacuumed the oriental rug claiming the living room floor.

In the summer I took up residence in the attic. In its cool, spacious recesses I pasted pictures from *Life* and *Look* on the walls. Under a loose floorboard I hid reams of poetry and my diary, which charted my anguished journey into adolescence. Most of all, I read books for comfort and salvation.

Leaning against the walls in that secret womb, I read *Ivanhoe*, *Vanity Fair*, *Tom Jones*, *Oliver Twist*. For two weeks my heart bled over the fate of Emma Bovary. One summer I lay stretched out on blankets there and read all of Jane Austen and Charlotte Brontë. Books simply saved me. Between their pages I transcended the horrors of my parents' marriage and the stark loneliness that regularly ambushed me.

My half sister, ten years my senior, was as gregarious as I was shy, and sallied like a storm cloud over my life. While I was a studious bookworm, she was a sparkling sunburst. Alienated from each other by parentage and age, we paid over and over for the sins of the father, the love of the mother. Surely I symbolized to my sister the end of the possibility of love between our mother and Mr. Robinson. This was my crime. Never could I prove my innocence.

And I came to this halting, uncertain sisterhood weighed down, nearly crushed by a self-doubt planted and confirmed by everything I ever saw. The idea that I could be beautiful was eclipsed by the specter of my sister's light skin and long hair. Whatever hope I nurtured of being loved for my looks was sabotaged by the straightedged shadow she cast. Never could I imagine her lonely. Never could I envision her afraid.

She was lithe and petite, while I remained chubby into my late teens. Doted on, adored because of her looks and effervescent personality, this acceptance from others reinforced her natural openness and won her not just friends but loyal fans. But I was not pretty. My skin was brown. My hair short. I was not loved by strangers, for, unlike my sister, I was afraid to take them at face value. The poems and daydreams that steadily erupted in my mind encased me in a world that belonged to me, that few could enter. This world was barrier and refuge. So I became a flower, wilting and gasping as I spiritually clung to walls and corners, terrified that my voice would be rejected or, even worse, merely ignored. Only as women were we able to fill the chasm that separated and bound us. But at seven, at ten, at thirteen I ran from her shadow.

The houses gave my mother her identity. They taught me carefully, unknowingly, about life. The second and third floors belonged to the roomers, and I spent disgraceful amounts of time rummaging through the whispers and shouts swirling behind those doors. Crouched on the floor outside Mr. and Mrs. Benton's room, I held my breath and heard her thin, whining voice rise in weak defense against a charge of stupidity or indolence spat out by her husband. She was a slender, birdlike woman, brimming with self-apology. Once a week she received a beating from her husband, who on Friday evenings at six o'clock shed the forced, jovial mood that carried him through the week as quickly as he removed his coat.

Outside Marlene Jasper's door, I was tutored in the essence of love and desire. Hiding in the darkened stairwell, I watched her boyfriend, a muscular, jovial construction worker, enter her room as Marlene murmured a surprised, soft hello.

A waitress in a nearby black-owned restaurant, she rushed noisily down the steps every morning at 7:15, hair uncombed, her gaze still wrapped in sleep. She was a hurricane streaking through the dining room, spilling coffee on her chest, moaning over unpolished shoes.

We were friends. She told me wry, funny stories about her family and her lovers as she cooked minute steaks and fried yams in butter, always enough for two, forcing me to eat dinner with her. Taking a fierce drag on a cigarette, much the way I imagined she would kiss a man, she gazed at her empty plate and wiggled her white-stockinged toes stretched out before her. There were days, she said, when something hurled her without warning into a world of bloody dreams and sleepless nights. "Sometimes I want to be somebody else," she told me, folding her hands to steady her voice. "My life is too small. Some days I feel its fingers wrapped around my neck." Then she folded her hands around mine. "But I'm scared to make myself up all over again. What if I find out God didn't give me enough to work with?" In hot pursuit of her life, it remained a phantom nonetheless, leaving her more puzzled than afraid. Even at twelve I could see why men loved her. Could not resist her husky laugh and the tender fragility of her face. And because I looked on that face more steadily than most, I saw and measured the pain embedded between the laugh lines creasing the sides of her mouth. So, outside her door I listened to bedsprings creak and mellow laughter and her voice, plaintive and bruised after all, ask about tomorrow and the day after that.

These were the people who moved with us to new homes when a house was relinquished to pay the debts my parents incurred. A caravan of people and furniture streamed out of the house like ants on those Saturday mornings. The moving vans resembled dinosaurs patiently waiting to be fed. Mr. Carter, who smoked a pipe and never came out of his room except to go to work and the bathroom, pounced on my mother with bitter complaints about a radio one of the movers had dropped. My father stood imperially amid the movement, surveying the activity with the eminence of a sheik watching his army follow him across the desert. And I, anxious and excited, carrying my goldfish bowl in one hand, my scrapbooks in the other, navigated the cluttered steps, wondering what this new house would teach me.

Finally my parents separated. On a spring afternoon so ripe it seemed incapable of betrayal, my mother packed two suitcases with our clothes and left the last house she owned. After an argument earlier that day, my father warned her to be gone by the time he returned in the evening. That night, standing on the porch of the house to which we fled, he explained to an old family friend, chagrin and forced laughter rumbling through his voice, "She knows I didn't mean it. I've said the same thing before and she never left. What happened today?" My father was as embarrassed as my mother was liberated by her act. That she had conspired in the destruction of her financial autonomy frightened her more than any threat he could make. She left my father not because of his warning but to find a phoenixlike second chance tucked away between the folds of her prayers.

Six months later we moved into a low-income housing project near George Washington University. The small, neat cluster of four buildings was surrounded by a phalanx of high-rise apartments that included the Watergate. My mother was fifty-five years old, vanquished but not defeated. Once a week my father came to our apartment to give me an allowance. Still in good form after years of practice, she coaxed her share as well. Battleworn, randomly scarred, my parents sat in the tiny kitchen savoring cups of coffee, appraising one another with the charity of grateful survivors of an emotional war. Sheer endurance had carved wisdom into the blood.

2

The April evening was muggy, our apartment listless beneath the darkness. "The Wild Wild West" filled the television screen as my mother sat on the sofa beside me, her arthritic knee propped on the coffee table. I watched the television set indifferently, my mind rummaging through a forest of more immediate concerns—the money for my senior class ring due next week, ordering a copy of the yearbook, where I should buy my prom dress. The heat was a blanket tucked under my chin. My skin was prickly with sweat. Kicking off my sandals, I started unbuttoning my blouse when the voice of an announcer interrupted the program to say that Martin Luther King had been shot in Memphis, Tennessee. My mother struggled upright and grabbed my arm, the wedding band she still wore cutting into my flesh. The flutter of her heart echoed in the palm of her hand and beat in spasms against my skin. Then fear crawled into the room with us. As she huddled me to her breast, I heard her small, whimpering cry. It sounded like hymns and eulogies dripping from the air inside a tiny, parched black church. In mourning already, she released me and wept softly, dabbing her eyes with a handkerchief.

The screen once again filled with scenes of the Old West. Listening to my mother's sobs, my body was set on edge by a raw, hard-edged anger that nothing in my life up to then had prepared me for. In that flashing, endless moment that had come on like a seizure, the blood of my belief in America seeped through my flesh and formed a puddle at my feet.

Dazed, disbelieving, I reached for the phone and began calling friends. They had all heard the news. Grief, sudden and deep, stripped us of speech. We clung mutely to the phone as though it were a life raft bobbing in a sea of cold, lapping madness. If we could just hear another's voice, even stilled and hurt like our own, then life might go on.

But Washington's ghetto, long voiceless and ignored, scrawled an angry cry along its streets, using bricks, bottles and torches for its song of sorrow. We knew no one man had killed the prophet. Rather, the combined weight of racism and an absence of moral courage had crushed him. A constitution ignored, laws denied, these were the weapons. America pulled the trigger. For three days and nights a fury of looting and burning cleansed and destroyed the inner core of the city. National Guard troops cordoned off the affected areas. President Johnson appealed on television for an end to the violence, a convulsion spreading across the country. Pacing the apartment, unable to go out because of the curfew, I sympathized with the rioters. A sense of impotence hounded me. I was still numb, catharsis beyond my grasp. I envied their freedom, rooted in the fact that nobody cared about their will or collective rage unless it spilled over the bounds of the ghetto. So the rage continued, taking shape in a death wish-like spiral that devoured only the ghetto, until it was spent and whimpers of regret replaced the shouts.

I walked the streets demolished by the riots a few days after the troops had left and the fires had died. Block after block was filled with only huge hulking store frames turned black from the flames, a damp smell of ashes hanging over each one. Pictures of Robert Kennedy still hung precariously in many store windows. Mountains of rubbish filled the streets. The "Soul Brother" signs that had been pasted on the store windows too late lay burned around the edges among piles of trash. The streets were choked with cars from the Maryland and Virginia suburbs, whites popping their heads out of car windows, snapping pictures.

The days after King's death saw an invisible barricade of tensions rise between the white and black students at Western High School. The black students did not know then that in a few months many of us would repudiate our white friends, no longer finding them "relevant." Finding instead their mere presence inconsistent with a "commitment to the struggle," which is what our lives became overnight. We did not know it, but some of us sensed it, caught tortured, shadowy glimpses of it in the changes festering like mines in the open, dangerous field we would enter upon graduating in June.

Andrea McKinley, small-boned as a deer, with a finely honed sharp wisdom, declared while we were leaving a civics class together that perhaps King's death was a blessing. Shrugging her thin shoulders, removing her glasses and rubbing her eyes, still red from tears, she said, "Let's face it. The movement has changed. He was from another era. He couldn't deal with the ghetto and I think he knew it."

"But how can you say that?" I screamed. "That's the most callous thing I ever heard." We stood in a corner of the crowded hallway, each hugging books to her chest as for support.

"Do you think that's an easy conclusion for me to come to?" Andrea asked, her look unmasked and pained. "What I'm talking about is a struggle with different rules. Rules that talk about what's really important—power, community control and identity. How can you talk about love to people who aren't even listening?" I had never imagined Andrea, so cool and intellectual, capable of such unflinching anger. At eighteen she had the demeanor of the Rhodes scholar she would later become. But at that moment her words sprang from the same place within her where my belief in America had snapped. Her tirade frightened me because she so precisely articulated my own doubts. It also inspired me because in the midst of a vacuum it offered hope.

"I'm going to spend the summer with my sister working with SNCC before I go to Oberlin," she said.

"That means you'll be going south?"

"Yes. Probably Mississippi."

"It's a battleground down there," I whispered, ashamed of the fear evident in my trembling voice.

"Marita, the front lines are everywhere."

"I feel like the world's turned upside down. I felt safe before. Now I don't know," I moaned.

"You don't feel safe because now you see the truth. You see how they lied. Integration. Civil Rights." She spat out the words harshly, her voice a train rushing out of control.

"Just yesterday we cloaked our anger in folk songs and fingers pointed at society," I said.

"Yesterday we had faith," she countered. "Yesterday we were willing to wait. I've got a class and I'm already late," she said hurriedly, glancing at her watch.

"We'll talk some more. We *have* to." Unexpectedly, she squeezed my shoulder, as awkwardly as I'd imagined it would be, and strode quickly down the hall.

In the deserted hallway the silence struck me like a gong. I stood there feeling very old. Unwise. And afraid to look over my shoulder. I wanted to cut the rest of the day, walk through Georgetown and look in the opulently decorated store windows, which were like wrapped packages of silver and gold waiting to be opened. I wished desperately to be frozen in time at that moment, with only this image in my brain. So I ran down the stairs and out the main entrance into a sun so radiant it stabbed my eyes. But even a sun that pure did not destroy the emotional turbulence that whispered in my ear the rest of that day.

3

When the knowledge came, its taste was sweet, bitter, eye-opening. A drug pulsing hot lead fire and ice through our veins. As clenched fists became the stars giving light to our night, the sound of "brother," "sister," our anthem, tumbled through full, determined lips. Turned the curse into a sacrament. Brow-beating, insistent, unforgiving, we took the offensive and for a moment turned white hatred into fear that drained blood from the face.

The tremors from the riots that convulsed the city had shuddered outward, piercing the solid certainty of the surrounding white world with bulging veins of doubt. Washington's private colleges hastily inaugurated scholarship programs for black high school students. A salve that absorbed the sting of the burn but left the wound startlingly clear.

I entered American University in the fall of 1968 as a Frederick Douglass Scholarship student, one of twenty-five from the inner city. The school sat nestled, almost hidden, in the comfortable upper reaches of northwest Washington, surrounded by embassies, cathedrals and the manicured, sprawling lawns of the city's upper class. To enter this world I caught the bus downtown and boarded it with black women domestic workers who rode to the end of the line to clean house for young and middle-aged white matrons. They gazed proudly at me, nodding at the books in my lap, slapping me on the back with a smile. In answer to the concern arching my brow, they told me with pursed, silent lips, "It's alright. It really is. I'd a done something else if I could've. Maybe been a teacher or something like that. But that was so long ago it don't even matter no more. So now you do it for me. But mostly do it for you." I accepted their encouragement and hated America for never allowing them to be selfish or greedy, to feel the steel-hard bite of ambition that could snatch their sleep at night or straighten their spines into a dare. They had parlayed their anger, brilliantly shaped it into a soft armor of survival.

The spirit of those women sat with me in every class I took at A.U. Once it was called "Jew U." Because hordes rejected by Columbia or Temple or N.Y.U. were accepted there. Their affluence, measured in shiny sports cars and perfect-fit clothes, was a vulgar parody. Overhearing their conversations, I imagined their homes—cluttered with gadgets and objects, kept orderly and clean by thrice-weekly cleaning women. So much comfort, so little grace. Listening to them, I felt as though I were choking and would run to open space for air.

But my teachers, I almost forgave them for being white. I learned from all of them. The best ones combined intelligence with wit and polished it to gleaming with caring and concern. I was curious, and impatient with dullness and stupidity, so the reading lists that brought tears of frustration to the eyes of some comforted me. For it was books that, one luminous summer I shall always remember, made me want to be Harriet Tubman instead of Tuesday Weld.

The summer before entering American University I had joined the fold of a group of Howard University students. Their uni-

forms were dashikis and blue jeans, and wildly unkempt, brazen
Afros. Charter members of SNCC, they had conceived and carried out the week-long shutdown of Howard that spring. With
their anger turned into calloused hands, they brusquely stripped
the lady of her white gloves and formal speech. Teeth now cut,
they took on the South, where they registered black voters. One
of them slapped a white sheriff and lived to weave that act into
the epic poem he saw his life to be.

I went to their parties, held in crumbling, once glorious apartments that surrounded the Howard campus. The infrared darkness hid the copies of *Liberator*, *Soulbook*, and *Black World*
stacked in piles underfoot. Malcolm X's eyes were spears aimed
at us from posters peeling from the wall. When the throb of Sly's
Stand! or James Brown's "Say It Loud (I'm Black and I'm
Proud)" was only a memory frosting the air, we formed a circle
and snake danced around the room, hands clapping, feet stomp-
ing, singing "Beep Beep Bang Bang Umgawah Black Power."
They taught me the new language, how to roll the words on my
tongue. How to drain meanings from the sound of each syllable
that no one would ever forget. Power. Revolution. We were prepared for war but would witness only skirmishes that left us
bloodied nevertheless.

I fell in love with one of them. He was a twenty-two-year-old
guerilla/singer/songwriter/black poet/revolutionary. Beneath
the dingy, wrinkled sheets of his hardly-ever-slept-in bed, tongue
sticky wet promising in my ear, he called me his African queen.
He bought a .22 caliber handgun the day he discovered his
phone was tapped and handled it like a water pistol. Quieting
my demands for time with him, he reminded me that dates were
what white girls wanted and, anyway, there was no place for so-
cializing in the midst of a revolution.

"Is there a place for love?" I asked, watching him hurriedly
pull on his shorts, wondering why his body turned corpse cold
when I cradled him in the moments after his frantic release.

"Only of black people as a whole. Not as individuals," he answered in the voice a man uses with a woman he secretly hates.
Then he smiled sadly, cupping my chin as though the realization
awakened an ache within him. At eighteen I could not suspect

how wantonly cruel his answer was. So I reached onto the platter for it. Swallowed it whole without tasting. It landed, heavy
and rebellious, in the pit of my stomach.

Since there would be no love in our revolution, I turned to
hate. It was easy enough to do. The Drum and Spear Bookstore
was opened that summer by several members of the group. Its
shelves stocked a whole range of books on black and African
studies, and they finished the stories my father had begun. I
learned of slave revolts, W. E. B. DuBois, black inventors, Carter
G. Woodson, Reconstruction, Jean Toomer, Timbuktu, the pre-
carious existence of freed slaves, Duke Ellington, Nat Turner,
Bessie Smith. Page after page put flesh and blood on the bones
of the past my father had kindled for me in spurts, which was
our own carefully guarded secret. This was all mine. This
wealth. This panorama of genius and endurance. And *they* had
kept it from me. Now I knew why. Invincibility swelled my
mind into a hard, gleaming muscle. And for an uneasy, tortured
time I surrendered to hate. Because of two thousand lynchings
and four little girls bombed in a Birmingham church. Because
they told me I was a slave but never said that once I'd been a
king. I became a true believer. I wrote a biweekly column for
the *Eagle,* the campus newspaper, in which I spread the gospel
of black consciousness, sat on a committee to implement a black
studies program at A.U., tutored black high school students and
wrote bristling black poetry that sizzled on the page. I was simultaneously driven and inspired. Dizzy with a confidence I'd
grown up believing brown girls never knew.

And we never suffered a moment of uncertainty, bludgeoning
critics into silence with our smug lack of humility. We knew, for
example, that what's *on* your head is as important as what's *in* it.

The natural was sprouting everywhere—dark sunflowers filling
a vacant field. No one could see my anger. But they could see
my hair. See that I was no longer a Negro girl. That I had chosen to become a black woman.

My mother, nursed in the folds of a town that once christened
its black babies Lee, after Robert E., and Jackson, after Stone-
wall, raised me on a dangerous generation's old belief. Because
of my dark brown complexion, she warned me against wearing

browns or yellows and reds, assuring me they would turn on me like an ugly secret revealed. And every summer I was admonished not to play in the sun, "'cause you gonna have to get a light husband anyway, for the sake of your children."

My mother would never acknowledge or even suspect her self-denial. It gripped her all the tighter for the carelessness of her vision. Ground into my pores, this was the same skin through which I breathed. The eye through which I saw myself.

Up until I was eighteen, however, every other Saturday I had entered a state of grace. Holding down a rugged corner of 14th and T, on a block given over to funeral parlors, ragged, unpretentious barber shops and fried chicken carry-outs, the La Femme Beauty Salon was part haven, part refuge for the women who packed its small rooms on Saturday mornings. Over the click of steaming curlers, they testified, embellishing the fabric of their lives, stretching it into a more agreeable form and shape. When it was full, the shop sweltered, holding the smoky odor of straightening combs thrust into jars of grease and applied with unflinching belief to coarse hair. Special attention was paid to "the kitchen," the hairline at the nape of the neck that harbored the most stubborn patches of hair curled into tiny balls of opposition. Pushing my ear back, the beautician would warn, "Now you gonna have to hold still 'cause I can't be responsible for what this hot comb might do."

Between customers, twirling in her chair, white-stockinged legs crossed, my beautician lamented to the hairdresser in the next stall, "I sure hope that Gloria Johnson don't come in here asking for me today. I swear 'fore God her hair is this long." She snapped her fingers to indicate the length. Contempt riding her words, she lit a cigarette and finished, "Barely enough to wash, let alone press and curl."

Despite those years—perhaps because of them—the day I looked in the mirror at my natural was the first day I ever liked what I saw. "There is everything," I thought. Nappy, defiant, my hair was a small cap tapering around my head. Without apology, my nose claimed the center of my face. Because of the bangs I'd always worn, I'd never noticed my brows, thick and velvety. My eyes were small diamonds. Perfectly cut. This was not the face I had always known. It was the face I refused to believe I had. I did not sojourn alone. My best friend, Wanda, was there. Two dark girls seeing themselves in the other. Don't explain. Had always been there. Waiting. Even before our minds wove together, strong-fingered hands clasped. Amidst the intellectual din, the emotional clutter ringing in the halls of Western High School, we had found one another. Imagination bound us stronger than love. Within its limitless borders we launched ships and love affairs, discovered lost worlds, made buildings and babies, found husbands, wrote letters and Broadway plays. We made ourselves up everyday. And because we dreamed of everything, we vowed to rule no possibility out of our lives.

In high school we read Sartre. In college we tossed him aside and reached for Mao and Che Guevara. Summer afternoons were spent stretched on her bed reading Don Lee and Gwendolyn Brooks. Together. Silent. We could read each other's minds. Spellbound listening to Coltrane's "My Favorite Things" over and over, each time a sacrament. Sweating, groaning, we raised the banner of blackness and, after the staff was firmly planted, became part of the women we would always be. And uh-huh, she would be an actress. I, a writer. A hundred loves, it seemed, unreturned, misunderstood.

Me: Jive nigguhs, all they do is rap. What's wrong with the brothers?
Wanda: Askin, "Sistuh, can you *love* a black man?"
Me: Hey, brother, can you *understand* a black woman?
Us: Laughter so close to tears it hurt.

I lay in the debris of a ruined love affair. Her voice, indignant, terrified in the face of my passion, my tears, charged, "Marita, you give too much."

"And you don't give at all," I slap back, hard. "You take them into your *bed* but never into your *heart*." She, the small bird chirping, afraid no one listens. Cautious. Fevered. The squirrel storing nuts of doubt. Love floods the rooms of her mind and she fills buckets with it, tossing the treasure out open windows. I am a stranger to half measures. With life I am on the attack, restlessly ferreting out each pleasure, foraging for answers, wringing from it even the pain. I ransack life, hunt it down. I am the hungry peasants storming the palace gates. I will have my share. No matter how it tastes.

My parents watched my transformation, stung by its ferocity and the fierceness of my allegiance to gods they had never known. My mother retreated into befuddled silence, watching me from the corner of her eyes, as though I were a stranger following her down a dark alley. My father said nothing for many months. Then, one afternoon, he waylaid me. He had stalked my moves, waited for my confidence to blossom before breaking it at the root. "I don't like what I see when I look at you now." His face was granite and my uneasy smile chipped away not one particle.

"What's wrong?"

"I want you to take off that makeup. I hate that lipstick, the mascara." His lips curled in disgust as he threw the words like sharpened darts.

"But, Daddy, there's nothing wrong—"

"And I want you to get rid of that natural."

"But why? You always taught me to be proud."

"Sure, I taught you to be proud. But you're still my little girl. My daughter." He said the words almost kindly, asserting his still pivotal role in a life I was wresting out of his hands. "You're not a woman yet, Marita. You have to do what I say."

His voice was stretched taut with a threat I was afraid to name. I had never even received a spanking from my father. Yet now, as I sat facing him in the front seat of his taxi, my heart was cringing, my hand reaching for the door. I tried to imagine what he would do if I refused. But the bitterness in his eyes, which accused me of betrayal because of my lurching journey into womanhood, left no room for denial. He searched my face for assent, for a request for forgiveness. I clenched my teeth and turned away from him, the window witnessing the tears sliding down my cheeks in thin ribbons that he could not see.

I obeyed him and the next day walked into the Soul Corner of A.U.'s cafeteria to stares and questions that peeled the skin from my cheeks. A few months later I got a work-study job at school.

No longer financially dependent on my father, I willfully disobeyed him and Afroed my hair once again. I was my own woman, I reasoned, forgetting, with a carelessness for which I would later pay, that I would always be his child.

4

In the winter of my junior year my mother suffered a massive stroke that left her in a coma until she died six months later. I came home one afternoon to find her lying on the bathroom floor, her breathing slight, eyes bulbous and glazed. Through the last days of winter, all of spring and midway through summer the same face stared at me, first in a private hospital and later in a nursing home.

I stayed on in our apartment, surrounded by reminders of her that fed the faint hope that she would live. By day I attended classes, conscientious and attentive. At night, in my mother's four-poster, I screamed, chanted, shouted her name through a symphony of tears. I beat the pillow with my fists, wrenching handfuls of sorrow from my heart. Stalking the bedroom in the darkness, I clutched the collar of my robe, rocking my body like a child, begging her to the rhythm of my movements to live. In the same darkness I fell to my knees, folding my hands in prayer. At dawn I lay tangled in sheets still damp from tears and sweat, my mind raw from the catharsis of the night before. Loneliness and despair branded me for all to see. Confusion and sheer terror lassoed my heart. My father and I were hushed into muteness by the specter of death. For we knew that my mother's death would force us finally to face and love each other alone, unaided by her conciliatory presence. In self-defense, we rarely spoke of her at length. We analyzed her condition in jargon assimilated from her doctor. But my mother, the woman we both loved—her life before, what it might be if she lived—was locked out of our consciousness.

My mother had scripted me to soar where she had glided. To migrate where she had chosen to nest. "I want you to travel," she told me, rubbing her swollen knee as she spoke. "Go to Paris, London. All those places you read about in your books. That's education too." In high school she proudly clipped my letters-to-the-editor published in the Washington *Post* and thrust them under the glance of her white employers. For my eighteenth birthday she gave me a subscription to the New York *Times*. In college she urged me to transfer to Antioch when an eager young liberal professor suggested the change. To my mother I had confessed every fear, every wish, every dream. And even as she lay dying, she offered me a way to shape the beginning of each day. I had watched her pace our apartment, her cane tapping the floor in a staccato beat as she worried, "I don't even have one house to leave you when I die. Not even one. And all those houses I had." She'd shake her head and look at me, her past unfolding in a flash on her face, saying, "I'll never forgive myself for that. No matter how long I live. Not for that."

Long intravenous tubes were taped to her arm and ran through her nose. I clasped her hand during my visits, rubbing her knuckles, and told her of classes, lovers, teachers, my father. My voice was a staunch prayer for life, competing with the sounds of traffic floating up from the street. I asked her advice, confided that I was afraid. I asked her, too, why she was dying. My mother's love had been imperfect but everlasting. Never had it failed me. "Before today," I said, tears glazing her fingernails, "I never thought it would."

Those monologues saved me for a while. But in the last months, when her body began to waste away—her arms flabby and fleshy, her cheeks hollow, the bones jutting like staffs beneath her skin—I could do no more than glance sideways at her and flee the room.

Finally, mercifully, she died. Her death, to my surprise, did not ennoble those who survived. Each of us whom my mother had loved withdrew into a numbing frigid sense of disbelief. From the vantage point of sorrow we were unable, unwilling to reach out to each other and confirm the reason for our grief. This lethal silence was more terrifying than the death that inspired it. Family ties, connections were cut. And not one of us bothered to wipe the blood from the floor.

From my mother's funeral I remembered most vividly the hollow sound of red-clay earth landing on her coffin. Tight-lipped, stunned, I watched her body being lowered into the ground. My faith in myself and everything else oozed from my body with the same precise, continuous force.

Deserting the apartment my mother and I had shared, I moved in with my mother's brother and his family. My uncle was a minister who was impassioned and articulate behind the pulpit. But confronted by my grief while wrestling with his own, he offered soothing platitudes that made no imprint on the surface of my misery. My grief, buttressed by an anger at the God to whom he urged me to pray, calcified, became a stone lodged firmly at the door of my heart. More than anything, I needed to curse, scream, rail in outrage. But there was no one to help me legitimize the exposure of such feelings. Never had I witnessed a precedent for such a naked, honest display. So I ran, sweating and panting, from the demands of fellowship. Neglecting others, I was neglected in return. Desiring only peace, turmoil snapped hungrily at my feet. My boyfriend, separated from his wife for a year, decided he loved her after all and tossed a hurried goodbye over his shoulder as he walked out of my life. Anger and love were the same. I was unable to speak to my father. Despair gagged the words. They easily gave up the fight. A feeble attempt at suicide, a call for help, the anguish ringing only in my ears.

One day I visited my mother's last house. When my mother and I moved out of it, my father inherited whatever financial rewards it could offer. Renouncing her last piece of property, my mother turned her back on my father and her past. My father had won a bittersweet victory—the house he had coveted so long, now his to manage alone.

That day the lawn was dry, overgrown, tufted into clumps, thick with weeds. Dirty, smudged windows callously eyed the street below. A pallor of neglect hung like a decisive shadow over each room. Although still occupied by tenants, the house smelled vacant, unused. My mother had taken the grand furniture that had imbued the house with so much authority. In its place mismatched chairs and tables stood, uneasy and self-conscious.

After my mother's death, my father left the house and moved in with a woman named Emily. She was a widow whose love for him renewed her interest in life. He came to the house now merely to collect rents, offering sporadic attempts at management. Beneath his hand the house sat orphaned, bereaved. The boarders were mostly single men and rootless, transient women. I walked through the house, my hand caressing the banisters caked with dust; stood on the splinter-filled back porch, its surface peeling paint and wood; paced the attic, now an empty cobweb-filled space. I opened the french doors to what had been my parents' bedroom. Rambling through the house, rummaging among its skeletal remains, I waited for fond lifesaving memories to flood my mind. But the memories did not well up. Did not grip me in a spasm that released my hunger and pain. As I sat before the fireplace where my father had told me of Nat Turner and Cleopatra, in my imagination I heard the house gasp. It released a long, surprised sigh that singed my blood, as memory had not, and crumbled almost gratefully into death. I left the house that day for the last time. Three years later, when I came back to the street, I found that a parking lot stood where the house had once lived. Only then could I cry, standing in the middle of the block on a hot July afternoon, sob-

bing uncontrollably as my eye scanned in disbelief row after row
of cars. Through my tears I wondered where they had buried
what used to be my life.

The summer of my mother's death was the beginning of a season of mourning. I mourned, too, the demise of the movement
that had shaped me. The leaders were all dead, jailed, ominously
quiet. It was over and no one could say what it had meant. Even
fewer had the courage to ask if it had been worth it. Some said
the dream died. Others knew it was killed by murderers, dressed
in revolutionary disguise, who stepped to the throne on its
corpse. I looked at the applications I was sending to graduate
schools—Columbia, Northwestern, Boston University—and saw
no imprint of the dream. I heard the passionless, bland speech
around me, voices asking for a job instead of the truth, and wondered if the dream had ever been real. The Future loomed, a
guillotine over my head, and I felt as prepared to shape it as I
had been four years earlier. The institutions we had created with
federal funds to design our revolution sat ravaged and bleak.
And since it could not survive the hostile winds abroad in the
land, I bundled the dream up, hid it in my heart and harbored it
there like a fugitive.

By the time I graduated from A.U., my father and I found the
words to touch one another. Pure, uncomplicated, startling in
their simplicity. The language of consolation stumbled across the
emotional obstacle course that divided us, landing happily on
the other side. The day of my graduation he stood awkwardly in
the foyer of Constitution Hall, with black-robed students, spring-
hatted mothers, picture-taking fathers swirling in waves around
him. He leaned heavily on a cane for support because of his arthritis. But dressed in a gray suit and black tie he was a panther
still. I spotted him from the other end of the foyer. Thrusting my
diploma into my cousin's hands, I waded through the crowd,
squeezing, pushing, hearing the hem of my robe tear, holding
onto my cap. We had talked by phone four times in the ten
months since my mother's death. Short, unsatisfying conversations that confirmed us as strangers. A craggy mountain of
unfinished emotional business hid us from each other's view—his
imperfect love of my mother, his affection for Emily, my jealousy

of her, our failure to share what grief we felt on my mother's death. But when I finally reached him, behind his glasses his eyes melted into unhesitating pride and acceptance. I hugged him, burying my face in shame and gratitude against his chest. I kissed his cologne-scented cheek. He was my father, whom I had never known how to forgive and, therefore, how to love. He was my father, whom now I had never loved more.

I had journeyed, tamed the wild terrain of my dreams. Had become a black woman citing a new beginning every day. Discovery. Anger. All made me the woman they told my mother she could never be. But was. Inside. Didn't know it. Cringed at the thought. I mined the dream. Pride was the treasure. Wiping blood from the lid, cautious hand lifting, looked inside. Saw the self always there. Affirmed. Made whole. Free.

11. *Journeys*

5

The summer after graduation from A.U. I worked as a reporting intern at the Baltimore *Sun*. The weather-beaten city struck me as a once proud dowager empress now fallen on hard times. Natives told me defensively of the city's once glorious past. But I saw few remnants of it in its close, neglected neighborhoods and dreary downtown.

The atmosphere at the paper reflected something of the city's loss of self-esteem, for although it was rated as one of the country's best, morale was virtually nonexistent. Everyone, especially, it seemed, those I learned from and came to respect, yearned for a job with the Washington *Post* if lucky, and the New York *Times* if blessed.

As a general assignment reporter I covered concerts, city council meetings, and wrote a profile of a black woman holiness preacher. I interviewed a wretchedly poor family of mi-

grants from West Virginia—in their tattered living room of crippled furniture, dust-caked plastic flowers, and children with
runny noses, sores and blisters—about their son's death in Viet-
nam. And then one dangerous, humid night the city's black
ghetto exploded. The match that lit the tinderbox—a white cop, a
black youth. I walked through the glass-strewn streets with a
white reporter assigned to the story, the sound of police radios
crackling, sirens twisting beneath the fretting night. Black faces
stared at me in surprise and dismay, hurling distrust. In defense
I clutched my reporter's pad and lagged behind my partner. I
felt like a shameless voyeur. I felt, most of all, like the enemy.

It was the police beat, however, that nurtured my distaste for
hard news and deadline reporting. For six weeks each day I
drove to all the police stations in Baltimore, checking out crimes.
Dank and shadowy inside, with asphalt hallways, they made me
think of hospitals or mental institutions. There was a desk ser-
geant, most often merely condescending, occasionally bellig-
erent, badgering a silent apology from me for my femaleness,
my blackness. No assignment demoralized me more. I watched
policemen drag in offenders, almost always black, who, because
they were, had little to lose as they cursed, kicked, resisted in
anger or intoxication. I never saw one black cop and came to appreciate that I hadn't. For the cops I saw every day walked as
though they were striding down a street in Dodge City. The camaraderie that bound them was tough and resilient, locking out
everyone who didn't wear a uniform.

Days off, I rented a car and drove to Washington, a short
forty-mile drive. I visited my father, our conversations intimate
and trusting. I envied the tranquillity that prevailed in the apartment he shared with Emily and wondered why he and my
mother had been unable to shape a similar peace. I asked him,
on one of those visits, if he had really loved my mother. "Sure I
did," he answered, surprise flickering in his eyes at the question.
Suddenly agitated, he rocked with more force in his rocking
chair and paused before adding, "I loved her very much. I just
didn't love her very well." Satisfied with his answer, he rocked
harder and harder, the chair creaking against the wood floor. "It
takes a long time to get some things right. And we just never had

the time." I knew this was as close as my father could come to the truth. "What, did you think I didn't love her?" he asked, indignation lurking in his voice.

"I just needed to hear you say it, daddy. I just needed to hear it come from you." I watched the struggle to decipher the hidden meaning of my words take form on his face. Soon he gave up, settled into the chair and rocked slowly, falling asleep before me.

Occasionally that summer, he wrote me letters. His script was still strong, but gnarled by the arthritis that had invaded his hands. Crossing the border into the zone of my father's love. The passage of time. Both helped me resurrect my mother from the grave. A year after her death, she was a torch lighting the path I had chosen. She had left me no houses but had bequeathed instead the legacy of a restless, courageous spirit. I followed her footprints north and they led me to New York City.

6

In New York I became an eagle, claws scratching the skin of its gritty sidewalks, wings spread, touching sun, casting shadows on the moon. Hunger glistened in my eyes, beat a war dance inside my veins. Unfamiliar, demanding appetites rumbled across the plain of my heart. I soared, wrestled with the clouds, the echo of my song trailing in the wind.

Wanda and I made the trek together, she to study acting at New York University, I to enter the world of journalism through Columbia's hallowed halls. Looking over our shoulders, the past seemed simple, sure. Turning to face the present, we remembered neither of us had trained for walking tightropes. But when we measured the distance of the drop, balance steadied our stride, stopped blood from the bitten lip.

We shared a one-bedroom apartment with six thousand New York City roaches. The space pressed around us, an inhospitable

womb. Drab, worn linoleum was pasted to the floors. The bathroom squatted in a corner of the sloping, L-shaped kitchen.
Dingy mustard-colored walls gave the space the atmosphere of a
cave. Two hundred dollars' worth of grates, bars, and locks at
the windows kept out robbers and the sun.

A young saxophonist from Atlanta lived next door in a room
the size of our toilet. Small and wiry, he throbbed with a talent
that bled in his eyes. His existence was improvised. One week a
gig with Mingus at the Village Gate, then two weeks of shoulders hunched, pounding the street for work. He told us we reminded him of his sisters back home. For him we were a touch-
stone, an echo of what he'd left behind, so he broke bread with
us many nights. Serene and comforting, he basked in the lush-
ness of our articulation, asking, "Sister mine, what was that
word? Run it past me again." Brows clenched in concentration,
he spoke best with his instrument. Watching his face open like a
Chinese fan, listening to the notes, we heard all we needed to
know. Love, hate, wrenched from safe harbor, pushed through
gleaming horn holding our awed reflection. His music knitted a
life, a lifetime in the shape of a rainbow across the kitchen's
stagnant air.

The frustrating, exhilarating getting of knowledge was what
New York City, and especially Columbia, was about. I left A.U.
with answers suitable for essay questions on midterm examina-
tions, but they crumbled, gasping and inadequate, under the
glare of an unpredictable "real" world. Columbia, however,
taught something ultimately more important. Columbia imparted
an attitude, and drilled not just confidence but fearlessness into
its chosen few. The most important thing I learned there was
how people get power and who decides who will share it. The
curriculum was an obstacle course that used New York City as
one large breaking story, a part of which we covered every day.
I scurried from one end of the city to another, covering a demon-
stration at the UN, interviewing undercover narcotics policemen,
questioning an aide to the mayor. Under the tutelage of Judith
Crist I studied film criticism. I learned the rudiments of televi-
sion-documentary production from Fred Friendly. We had audi-
ences with Tom Wolfe, Dan Rather and other media celebrities

during Monday-morning colloquiums. Our first assignment was the fall 1972 elections. The entire student body covered election headquarters and voting stations, staying at the school till 3 A.M. to produce a morning-edition paper and a broadcast of the results. One girl withdrew two months into the fall term, pasting a letter on the door of the student lounge saying she'd rather write poetry in the Village than meet inhuman deadlines on Morningside Heights.

The twenty-five black students were caught in a vise of warring expectations. We were eager and ambitious yet scoffed at the rah-rah old-boy loyalty our professors demanded. We hungered after the same prestigious jobs after graduation as our white counterparts, but we had cut our teeth on Black Power and wanted to enter the white world without having to check our identities at the door. One blunt, hard-nosed professor looked at the fifteen students in his class one morning and, counting four blacks among them, folded his hands and solemnly announced that the black students at Columbia had been admitted largely on the basis of race. We protested, petitioning the dean, who assured us politely but unconvincingly that the views expressed by one professor did not represent the school. At our weekend parties we promised each other we'd never sell out for the *Times* or *Newsweek*. We'd expose. We'd crusade. The smartest among us knew we had no other choice.

While I chiseled at the city's granite exterior for answers, Wanda erected a prop-filled stage from which she made her plea. Wanda lived a life on the stage that allowed her to evolve into a miracle. Her tiny frame contained an energy that blossomed once she donned the personality of a "character." To watch her perform was to hear the heartbeat of secrets that went unveiled when she played the more difficult role of herself. She was not shy. Rather, she simply treasured her gift and lived in fear of squandering herself in some fraudulent act from which she might never recover. The mother and aunt who raised her were puzzled and more than a little frightened by her choice of careers. They feared losing her to a world where illusion and fact melded into a poetry so precise it could undermine any reality that had come before.

Her talent was slowly, inevitably glazed with ambition. She studied theater at N.Y.U., breathing the same intense, self-conscious atmosphere that spread like a fog from one end of Manhattan to the other. I attended some of her workshops and auditions. She had abandoned hesitance and was learning how to advertise herself by the way she entered the room, glancing disinterestedly at the director as though she already knew she had the part. She calculated so deftly—mastering facial expressions before the bathroom mirror—that she appeared totally natural. Her aura on these occasions was so asexual, so assured, that it became enticing.

She was always *on*, preparing for, worried about an impending tryout or audition. Three months after we arrived she landed a lead role in an all-black production of a play by Tennessee Williams. The play ran for four weekends in the basement of a West Side church, and her notices were good. The last night of the production I surprised her in her dressing room with a bouquet of roses and a bottle of champagne. Raising a plastic champagne glass in tribute to her, I said, "This may be the closing night, but it's just the beginning." I'd gotten a check for $150 the week before from the Baltimore *Sun* for two book reviews, so I splurged, taking her to dinner at an East Side French restaurant we'd promised ourselves when we could afford it. In the taxi her ebullience began to dissipate into moodiness, and by the time the waiter brought our order of snails she was visibly depressed.

Slumping against the back of the booth, she looked at me accusingly and asked, "Do you know how many actresses there are in New York?" Realizing the question was purely rhetorical and sensing her mood, I did not answer but looked instead in my lap and began folding the crisp linen napkin. "Do you know how many *black* actresses there are in New York?" she pursued.

"Wanda, the lights are down. Your makeup's off. Just spit it out. I'm not an audience. I'm your best friend." She turned her eyes on me like searchlights and then suddenly looked away, as if caught in a lie. "What is it?" I asked.

"I'm burnt out. Drained. I feel so down and I don't know why."

"I guess it's just a natural letdown at the end of a production," I ventured.

"It's not the production. It's what I had to go through to get the part. And now it starts all over again."

"What're you afraid of?"

"Of trying too hard," she said, pulling the words like teeth. "Giving too much."

"But isn't that what acting is about?"

"Yes. And that's what scares me. I'm afraid one day I'll have to sell more than I can buy back. Just to get a part."

"I know the competition's tough but—"

"It's not just tough. It's murderous. You just don't see the blood on my hands."

Three months later Wanda auditioned for a part in a play about three generations of black women, written by a young black playwright who'd won several prestigious awards the year before. The play was to be produced by a well-funded black theater company that trained black dramatic talent. She didn't really think she had a chance of getting the part. Mostly she wanted the experience of performing before what constituted New York's black theater establishment. The days before the audition she spent in the throes of incredible mood shifts, one moment nonchalant, the next nervous, filling the apartment with smoke from the cigarettes she only puffed when she was afraid. She was playing a mental game I shrank from watching. Convincing herself the audition was unimportant because she feared giving a poor performance, she nonetheless primed herself for success—the only frame of mind that would allow her to act with any conviction.

She was chosen as one of three finalists for the role. The evening after the audition the director called her. She went out and didn't come back until the next morning. She refused to talk about where she'd been, what she'd done. For the next week she waited for a call telling her she had the part. Finally she called the company and was told another actress had been chosen.

"I don't even know why I did it," she told me that night. "Why it happened." She was curled up on the sofa bed, her body coiled as tight as a snail's. "He had this loft in Chinatown, furnished with wall-to-wall carpeting and nothing else. And that's where it happened. On the floor beneath a giant framed lithograph of Josephine Baker. I wanted to talk about the play. My concept of the character. Do some improvs. He let me do that for a while. I could see he was bored, but I kept on talking. I was scared not to. I felt maybe if I talked I could control what was happening. Then he drained his wineglass, stood up and stripped. I was so stunned I could hardly breathe. He started unbuttoning my blouse and I was still talking. He unhooked my bra. His hands were cold and I could tell they meant to shut me up, but I couldn't stop. He put his hands inside my panties and pulled me closer to him. I was talking about A.U. and staring over his shoulder at plaques and awards he'd won for directing. By then I was talking about high school and he was easing my panties and slacks off. He pulled me onto the floor. And all through it I kept talking and he never once asked me to stop. When he came—jerking in this horrible, angry spasm, with his hands pinning me to the floor—I was talking about being ten years old and playing Mary in the Christmas pageant. I felt his come running down my thigh and it was then that I realized that all the time I'd been talking I'd been crying too." She lit a cigarette and took a long drag. "As soon as it was over he fell asleep. For two hours I lay beside him like a corpse, afraid to move, afraid not to. Then I got dressed and left. I spent the rest of the night walking around Times Square. I wanted to be around lights and the people as lost and hungry as I was. I didn't know I was that hungry, Marita. What do I do now?"

"The fact that it happened doesn't mean you wanted it."

"But that's what I don't know. Did I want it to happen? That's terribly important for me to know."

"Maybe it's best that you stop trying to find out—for a while anyway."

"So what do I do now? What can I do?" she persisted, casting me, as she often did, in the role of the wiser of the two of us, a role I resented, felt ill-equipped to play but performed nonetheless.

"Wanda, I don't have an answer. The only thing I can say to

you is start all over again. From scratch. That's the only thing anyone ever told me. It's the only thing I can tell you."

But she didn't start over. Instead she dropped out of school and registered with an employment agency, floating from one low-paying clerical job to another. "I just need time to think," she explained. "About me and what I've chosen." This was her penance—doing work she hated, severing ties to a world she loved but increasingly feared would destroy her. Then she discovered she was pregnant. I went with her to an East Side clinic for the abortion. That evening she rested in bed, sipping herb tea and eating crackers. Finally she cried—for the director, herself, the baby, three months as a file clerk, and the decision she couldn't run from much longer. I let her cry and then sat on the bed beside her, pressing tissues into her hand. "Why don't you think about getting back in it, Wanda? Take some night courses, just to see how you feel. All that ugliness is behind you now. It may haunt you, but it won't destroy you."

"Is that a promise?" she hopefully asked.

I hugged her and closed my eyes to make the wish come true. "It's a promise. I promise you that."

7

The men I met in those first months were sharks—teeth and warm, moist breath on my shoulders. Egos, neon signs glowing after dark. Their affection, ice carved into animals I never saw in any zoo.

With Paul, a South African graduate student majoring in economics who really wanted to be a playwright, I shared nights in bed, sipping wine from plastic cups, trading metaphors, bartering lust. He read scenes from his plays, I divulged my poems. Leon Thomas and Betty Carter provided rhythmic counterpoint. His clipped British accent, pushing my name out the corner of his mouth too fast, turned it into "Martha." The imp dancing a jig in his eyes ignited a respect for him in me that survived fall and winter, and other lovers as well.

Then there was Michael. Benign, but hardly harmless, he wore an impenetrable mask of control. He was a photographer whose camera freeze-framed the majesty of a child's smile, the stillness of a raindrop, the faces of black farm workers—all with equal ease. Spontaneous. Aesthetic. A stickler for perfection and order. He opened doors for me, helped me with my coat, effortlessly popped the cork off bottles of Beaujolais 1962 and settled down with me before his log-filled fireplace. His was the apartment of a man who loved mostly himself. Scandinavian furniture. Blow-ups of his photos framed and looming from the walls. A well-stocked, spacious darkroom. Possessions. A bookcase lined with trinkets gathered during years spent wandering and discovering abroad. Our conversations were tournaments. My energy and wit inspired him. It also was a raw wind chafing his cheeks.

We spent Saturday afternoons in antiquarian bookshops. Held hands, clutched waists, strolling the halls of the Museum of Modern Art. He introduced me to his father, a musician and collector of African art who, as we left his apartment, slipped a brass ring from Dahomey into my palm. Michael gave me the key to his apartment, bought me an emerald ring and then told me not to fall in love with him. "Don't try to love me, okay? Promise me you won't do that."

"Michael," I laughed, striving for a nonchalance I was suddenly afraid I would never feel again, "that's straight out of a B movie."

"I have nothing to give you that you could use. That would help you." Answering the question on my face, he said, "Oh, I'm not being modest. I'm trying to be fair."

"I don't want your justice. I want your body," I leered at him, hugging his shoulders.

Easing out of my hold, he stared at me as though I was an intruder who'd just broken into his apartment. "I'm not kidding. Don't try to make me give you more than I already have."

He was too late and, as I now saw, not as smart as I thought. If he were, he'd have known that I'd launched my attack months ago. In love I used guerilla tactics, priding myself on speed, the ability to surprise, to withdraw and remain planted in each region of the heart simultaneously. Michael was a mountain I would scale to chip away the concrete exterior, excavate his emotions and carve a grand artifact of love and faith.

But he had repulsed onslaughts like mine before. Had mastered camouflage. Had survived even the surprise attack. Soon we both knew there would be no truce, no white flag, only one of us poised and dangerous over the other, a cold bayonet against the neck's blushing skin.

In the midst of this battle my father died. The night of his birthday he'd gone out to a party. Returning home at 2 A.M., he fell asleep on the sofa. Sometime during the early morning he suffered a fatal heart attack. I went to Washington for the funeral and rode in the hearse beside Emily. Being a woman of homespun grace, she lacked my mother's grandeur and will. A cherublike innocence shivered in her countenance. Tense and sobbing, she sat beside me, hugging her corner of the seat. Then her voice, yearning, accusing, turned my face to hers. "I loved your father. More than anybody I ever knew. You don't believe that, do you?"

When I had visited my father—Emily in the kitchen cooking, in the bedroom reading her Bible, putting on her hat to go to the store, knitting a shawl in her rocking chair, standing next to a window watering wandering Jew and spider plants, making tea for my father, ironing his shirts—I had seen her love. Sacrificial, it was a shimmering halo over my father's head. I had seen his contentment. For she was above all a woman who inspired a self-satisfied acceptance of her humility. I looked at her now—the late January sun brilliant, harsh, bouncing off the window over her shoulder—and said, "I knew you loved my father. And I never forgave you for that. I was always afraid of you. Afraid he'd love you more than me." I remembered my condescension on those visits, flaunting my intimacy with my father, pushing her aside with the hand of my possession. "I'm sorry I never liked you," I whispered sadly. "But you loved him more than I could stand."

"You're only a child and you don't know it," she said gently. "All he wanted was for you to love him a little more, and you could've loved me as well."

My father's death stripped me of a connection to the past, made it impossible to dare think of the future. I had dreams in which I fell through black holes in space, my voice echoing against the walls of a world deserted—where everyone was dead but me. Scavenging through the rubble of memories, I searched for the crime that had provoked this latest punishment. Existence was a demanding, sickly, never-wanted-in-the-first-place child, crying without reason or end. All the resilience and tenacity my father had helped me shape after my mother's death shattered, jagged and dangerous, slitting the seams of my contentment. Loss was a starched habit I struggled to remove. Now, I wanted more than anything else to die, but my parents had only taught me how to live.

Terrified, I returned to New York and for a few more weeks Michael and I danced politely away from one another in ever larger circles. He offered condolences and little else, shrinking from the scent of loss, a deadly perfume that clung to my skin. I wanted not sympathy but salvation. So we wrestled with our feelings—overripe plums festering beneath a naked sun, dripping the juice of regret and indecision. And then one day we said good-bye in hollow voices that did not reverberate with remembered love but trembled instead with embarrassment and the shock of fatigue. Over the days and weeks that followed I vowed not to lose love again.

8

My closest companion at Columbia was Paula Jackson. She was a shooting star and her energy warmed everyone who approached. Tough, cynical and wise, she was among the most feminine of women. She draped her body around a man's with the sound of her voice. Simultaneously she was the first "uppity" woman I ever met. In the fall and winter her passion had been for actors and musicians, so we attended loft parties on the Lower East Side and on the borders of Chinatown. As spring approached, she attached herself to a group of African diplomats and students—mostly Nigerians.

One Saturday evening we attended a farewell party for a prosperous Nigerian businessman who, after a dozen years in the States, was going home. The send-off brought out a cross section of the New York Nigerian community, from students and businessmen to diplomats and wives. Paula blithely fended off numerous dance partners as she kept her eye on the guest of honor, who was also her lover. Between sips of champagne and distracted conversation with me, she measured how close he stood to his wife and followed his circumnavigations around the huge chandeliered room, shaking hands and saying good-bye to colleagues and friends. He conspicuously, studiously ignored her. At midnight, just as the party was winding down and we had both given up hope of making a connection with any attractive males, two young men walked in. Paula knew one of them, Vincent, an insistent, oft-spurned lover who doggedly appeared when she least expected it. He immediately spotted Paula and came over to join us. Vincent's friend was of medium height and his copper-colored skin shone as though it had been lovingly, meticulously polished. His small eyes were filled with a mixture of shyness and arrogance as he stood before me, enveloped in the aura of supreme confidence that blossomed around all the Africans I had ever met. While Paula shepherded Vincent onto the dance floor to perform, throwing wild taunts with her body at her lover standing on the sidelines, I talked to Vincent's friend. His name was Femi Ajayi. In speech flavored with a halting British West African accent that made everything he said sound irresistible and solemn, he told me he was studying for a master's degree in architecture at Cornell. The palms of his hands were the color of brownish-red clay, tough and calloused. But the skin covering them appeared soft, the nails perfectly manicured and shaped. I had never seen hands so mapped in contradictions. An hour later, when he took my elbow to lead me to the coatroom, his presence was obtrusive and irresistible. Outside my apartment slivers of moonlight rained into the darkened hallway while he stroked my face, his hands engraving promises on my cheeks.

On our first date the tight petals of his reserve uncoiled, forced apart by my eager scrutiny. "Tell me everything about Nigeria. Then tell me everything about you."

He etched verbal pictures of his father, who was a chief, the man's eight wives and many children, his country—at once underdeveloped and lurching toward modern ways—and, most vividly, what he would do when he returned to a place pulsing so audibly through his bones and blood. I felt negligible in the shadow he cast. I'd read about my past and now it sat across from me in a steak house, placid, and even a bit smug. He appeared unaccustomed to hesitation and read his life as though it were a map. I wanted to know how he maintained such composure in the face of a life so frequently arbitrary and cruel. So, closing my eyes tight, I rubbed my fingers across his hand. "What're you doing?" he asked.

"I want some of your confidence to rub off on me," I said, opening my eyes slowly.

Flattered, he broke into childish laughter. He thought I was kidding.

His lovemaking was fervent, blunt, like being swept up in a hurricane, and he looked upon me with the delight of a child, surprised and grateful that I was his. And I became his with an ease that only confounded me later, when there was no turning back. He did not evoke in me an immediate rush of passion but elicited instead a sense of safety. We alternated weekend visits, with me taking the bus to Ithaca or him driving to Manhattan. He subscribed to *Fortune*, made the dean's list, and crammed his pockets with scraps of paper on which he had outlined lucrative businesses he wanted to establish when he returned to Nigeria.

His ambition and drive easily won my heart, and yet one evening, in the middle of a phone discussion, he said, "I love you."

I had heard the words before from others. This time I did not have to strip them down to trembling flesh. Yet I retreated from this sudden onslaught of affection. Laughing assuredly, I responded, "You don't mean you love me; it's too soon for that." I could barely hear his breathing on the other end, but I saw him fold up the words and tuck them away. It would be months before he would confess them to me again.

His older brother, Babatope, was an intern at Kings County Hospital Center. One evening Femi took me to meet Tope, who carefully, casually scrutinized me. They had different mothers but had inherited the same solid, jutting chin and closely carved, receding hairline from their father. Talking with Tope was like warming one's hands before a log fire as winter scratched at the windows. As his younger brother, Femi accorded him the respect of an elder.

My questions to Tope about his studies, reactions to the United States and details of the Biafran war relaxed him and from the start made him an ally and friend.

"Your interest in Africa is unusual," he observed. "Most of the blacks I have met show no interest at all, or are totally ignorant of the facts. One man at my job asked me if we still eat people in Africa. Another wondered if we lived in trees. It's the whites who invite me into their homes, who are eager to know about my country and not make fun of it."

"I believe you," I agreed lamely. "But it's a long, complicated story, why we're this way."

"I will listen," he said, moving from the dining room table to the sofa where I sat. "I am an African and time is not everything to me."

I told him about Tarzan movies, Africa jokes, slavery, and a past I'd dug to find like a determined, driven prospector.

"But we do not know these things," he said wondrously. "We cannot know how you have suffered."

I concluded, "And to some of us you appear so proud. Too proud. And some of us hate you for it."

He leaned back against the sofa. "We, too, have suffered because of the whites. But our beliefs remain. Each generation reaffirms who we are. And who we are never changes." He paused for a moment, considering. "Then my cousins here have done well," he concluded, "if only to have survived."

Femi joined us and we talked late into the night, sparks of revelation and admission of sin bouncing among us as we moved toward understanding.

At the parties we attended Femi's friends devoured me with lavish, open smiles and conversation. They were aggressive but never rude. The women, clustered in a corner of the room away from the men, nursed babies and wiped the greasy hands of toddlers. Their side of the room sang with the music of gossip and complaint. Friendly enough, but impenetrable, the women turned away after Femi introduced me, clicking their tongues and worrying inside, "Another American. Where are their men?"

An ambassador, I laid claim to the entire room and wandered between camps, the only way I knew how to live.

His was the most beautiful back I had ever seen. Like his hands, resisting, stubborn, yet tender. The unblemished skin a mirror reflecting my face. I straddled his waist, massaging him, our favorite ritual. No gift satisfied him more. A border had been crossed, for he had learned to make love to me instead of taking me. My friends had met him, approved and were warmed by the rays of my happiness. Lying on his back now, head resting against his arms, I still straddled his waist, my fingers toying with his nipples—dark eyes in the face of his chest. Our eyes met and I said the words that had pressed steadily for release against the doors of my restraint. "I—I love you." For a long moment the words dangled in the air. A smile of triumph flashed across his face, threw streamers into his eyes. He savoured the taste of my words, as though he'd known to expect them, but was surprised at their arrival just now.

"It's not enough for you to love me. You can't love just me alone. You must love my mother, my father, my family."

A second of fear raced like an electric bolt through my body as my skin bristled with courage. "I will love them," I said, already feeling the warmth as in my imagination I was pressed against their bosom. Felt them laying hands upon me, anointing me with the cool waters of acceptance. Already I had left this cosmic loneliness, the disconnectedness snapping at my heels. "Yes, I will love them." I closed my eyes and remembered all the men I had loved, too busy, too afraid to take me, incomplete, and make me whole. I calmed his puzzled expression, saying, as I kissed his cheek, "Yes. I will love them, and I will always love you."

"It will not be easy," he warned, sitting up for emphasis. "Americans do not know this love. In my family we owe everything to everyone else. Can you accept that burden?" A fault line rumbled across my conviction. "Can you pay a debt like that? Honor me with that kind of love?"

"Yes," I whispered, deliverance wiping beads of sweat from my brow. His hands gripped my head and his look, so direct it branded my face, said the words of love—retrieved, unfolded, still new.

9

After graduating from Columbia I got my own apartment and worked as an editorial assistant in a large publishing company. At Columbia I had majored in magazine writing, finding it the most comfortable journalistic niche. The magazine article allowed me to explore without deadline pressures and in depth a subject or personality. An idea could become an adventure as I researched, interviewed, and finally wrote. I wanted to spend a year free-lancing, but I needed a job to pay the rent. At the publishing company I was essentially a secretary. The job, however, left me free in the evenings and on weekends to research and interview. Writing became a vehicle through which I mined New York for virtually every kind of experience and knowledge it offered. For the *Amsterdam News* I wrote theater reviews and personality profiles. For *Essence*, a black woman's monthly magazine, I interviewed black feminists for a piece on black women's liberation.

The women's convictions about the psychosexual and economic oppression of black women were passionately held and eloquently stated. Their assertions challenged my beliefs yet reinforced everything experience and reality had taught me. In talking to the women I journeyed into a region of myself that had long been sealed. By the time I finished the article I had evolved once again. I looked stereotype and myth dead in the eyes and vowed they would never claim me as victim.

Next, *Essence* assigned me to write an article on rape. Women's liberation groups around the country were marshaling public opinion against the nation's rape laws, which, more often than not, resulted in few convictions and discouraged rape victims from reporting the crime, fearful of humiliation in a courtroom. For three months I interviewed feminists, lawyers, psychologists, rape victims and even convicted rapists. The world that this story opened up to me was as depressing and fearful as the previous piece had been thought-provoking. I had to confront the pain of my subjects—the victims and victimizers—as well as my own fears. I dug deep and produced the strongest piece I had yet written.

After a year and a half I had learned to strut, balance the city on my nose, juggle it with one hand and lay a thunderous slap on its ever-extended palm. The Big Apple was a friend who sheltered and possessed me, shadowboxing and teasing. New York was home as Washington had never been, could never be, just as Greensboro had touched nothing of my mother's soul.

The aggressive, guttural sound of Yoruba swirled around me. Femi and I had come to visit his brother, Tope, and stayed for dinner. Soon the apartment held a dozen other Nigerians. Straggling into the kitchen, they came out with plates burdened with mounds of rice and African stew. They stood and sat in small groups, laughing and arguing, the musical foreign sound bursting through their lips. I had learned to listen to the language as music weaving a song I would one day begin to understand. They lapsed into Yoruba often, interspersing it with bursts of

English. Beside me Femi leaned forward to better hear what his cousin Sola was saying. In a second the words accelerated; relentlessly crowding around me, they became a hulking, heavy-breathing presence. Animation and laughter stamped the others' faces in response to the cascade of words I could not understand. The words became an iron door creaking in my imagination. I heard it slam shut, locking me out of their world. Retreating, I sank into the soft cushion of the sofa, wishing desperately to disappear.

Moments later Tope perched on the arm of the sofa beside me. His eyes apologized for the words, still vigorous, muscular, striding around us, still masked to me. "How are you?" he asked gently. "We haven't talked much since the others came in."

"I'm okay," I lied, smiling foolishly. We sat together, talking against the sound of the others. He enfolded me where no one else had. When we were about to leave, I stood at the door and he pulled Femi aside, whispering in his ear. Femi shot a glance at me and responded angrily in self-defense. Tope shook his head, held up his hands and pointed to me.

In the car Femi said nothing, his body ramrod straight, the chill emanating from it making me shiver. Finally he asked, "What did you tell my brother?"

"I didn't have to tell him anything. He understood."

"Understood what?"

"How locked out I felt." My voice began to tremble at the memory.

"What do you expect us to do?" he lashed out angrily, "speak English all the time? It's not our language. No one was trying to lock you out. We were talking among ourselves."

"And what am I to do?" I spat out the words, anger overtaking the hurt. "Why can't you explain, translate, include me? Is that so hard?"

"Yes, it is. I won't promise to do that every time."

"*Every* time? You never do it. When the conversation turns to Yoruba, do I suddenly disappear?"

"I'm a man. My job is to be that. Not to cater to and pet you in public." His words punched, slapped, kicked me. "If you want to speak my language, go take a class somewhere." He was driving with one hand, orchestrating his anger with the other. "It's your job to learn it, not mine to teach you."

We arrived at my apartment. The motor idled as he fidgeted impatiently, waiting for me to get out.

The next day Tope called. I told him about our fight. "Let me call Femi now," he said. "I will talk to him."

"Why can't he talk to me? It's our problem," I protested.

"He will say to me what he can't say to you."

"Why?"

"Because I am his brother. And I am a man."

"But Tope—"

"You will hear from him," he promised, and then he hung up.

Femi called, and in the wake of his hello an endless pause blossomed, filling my nostrils, snatching my breath. I could not wait for what I knew he would not say. "Come be with me tonight," I pleaded.

"I will be there."

Among these Nigerians I had found a haven. The turbulent waters of my recent past had washed me ashore. Here I would find peace. Here I would find love. I told Femi of my parents' deaths, mentioning them almost in passing. Grief had shrouded me so long, I only wanted to shape a rebirth of hope. Death had held me hostage. Now I wanted to find life. Despite Columbia and the beginnings of a career as a writer, I had felt worthless. My self-concept fragile, my ego torn into shreds by a dual loss. My parents' deaths seemed to confirm me as undeserving of happiness. But in Femi's world I became a woman who loved and was loved in return. Eagerly I strained to understand and meld into a community grounded in a sense of family and connectedness—the ethic that would heal my wounds. Femi, his friends and family were a clan. And they had taken me into the fold.

Tope's wife had arrived from Nigeria. Months earlier he sent a friend home to find him a mate. Letters and pictures were exchanged. Money sent for the girl to join him, a letter to the U.S. Department of Immigration stating that she was his fiancée, and finally she came.

I was part of the greeting party that accompanied Tope to
J.F.K. International Airport. A short, rotund girl, Nike walked
through customs carrying enough luggage for an army. The
group loudly admired her blue and yellow traditional Yoruba
dress, consisting of a top and yards of cloth swathing her
from the waist to the floor. A stiff brocade *galae* wrapped her
head. Heavy gold earrings dangled seductively. More gold spar-
kled at her neck and arms. When her eyes met Tope's she smiled
modestly and bowed to the floor as a sign of respect. "Welcome
Iyawo (wife)," he said, his voice quaking and small. Outside the
airport they posed for pictures. For the camera Tope fumbled to
find her mouth, and she let her arms awkwardly drape his shoulders.

Femi's car was part of the caravan driving back to Brooklyn
for a welcome party. Sola sat in the backseat. Tope was my ally,
but Sola had become my surrogate brother. Serious, intellectual,
he taught African history at Hunter College part time while
working on his doctorate. He had introduced me to the political
gospels of Nkrumah and Nyerere, and though he traveled to
Nigeria once a year, he swore that he would never return there
to live because of the corruption and stagnation that greeted him
on every trip. Now stuffing his Yashica back into its case, he
clicked his tongue loudly. "I wish Tope luck with this girl, Femi,
but I swear I will never marry a woman I have had no hand in
choosing." I wondered if this pronouncement was for my sake. I
had met Sola's girl friend, an attractive schoolteacher who was
the mother of a five-year-old daughter. She and Sola had been
involved for two years. She was in love with him and hoped they
would marry once he finished his studies. But Sola had warned
me already that though he loved Margaret, he could never marry
her. "My family would never accept another man's child. They
would believe that she must still love the child's father."

"What about you?"

"I'd believe it too."

"But, Sola, that's ridiculous," I protested.

"It's not ridiculous, it's our custom."

Whenever I confronted the hold of tradition on their actions
and beliefs, and their contradictory straddling of two worlds, I

felt a surge of fear. I sat there in the car next to Femi, wondering what kind of marriage Nike and Tope would have. Would they spend their first night together trading small talk? What happened if they discovered they were not compatible? I shuddered and drew my coat around me tighter.

Smoke from Sola's cigarette wafted around my head.

"We are modern men," he continued. "We are not our fathers."

I turned towards Femi. "Would you send home for a wife?"

"Last year I did."

My stomach threatened rebellion, and the chill I'd just felt gave way to feverish warmth. "What happened?" I blurted out, needing to fill even a hint of silence with speech. For if silence reigned even for a moment I might shatter as finely as glass.

"It didn't work out."

"But you would've married her if it had?"

"Yes."

I now wanted to know everything. "Who was she?"

"A girl from Lagos," he answered, his voice becoming edgy and impatient. "A friend of one of my brothers. I wrote home, telling him I was lonely here. That I had turned thirty and knew it was time for me to marry. I asked him to send me a wife."

I recalled pictures I'd seen of Femi with previous girl friends, some white, some black. Pictures dog-eared at the edges, yellowing inside the plastic frame of his wallet or pasted onto pages in his photo album. Pictures of him with his arm around the girl's shoulders, both of them smiling. Girls like me. Who chose their own husbands. Who thought love was a miracle that bound them to him. Girls, I was sure, he'd had to strive to know and understand. Yet, when he wanted to marry he sent home for a wife. A stranger whose body had curves and secret places he would discover only after the fact. A woman he did not know. Perhaps did not need to know. A woman of his culture to whom he would owe no explanations. A faceless, anonymous, obedient woman. I looked at him again and did not recognize him at all.

Sola loudly clicked his tongue in the backseat again. "Look at Remi and Wole last year. Three months after the girl arrived, Wole came home one day and found her gone. She's run off and he hasn't heard from her since. I tell you, it's time these customs changed. How can an educated man marry a woman he doesn't know? And you, Femi, are as crazy as Wole to even have thought of it. Bless the day you stopped writing that girl."

In the end Nike did not make a good wife. She was a loner, preferring her own company to the fraternity of the other women, who occupied themselves with jobs, part-time study, having babies and running their homes. The other women were born to be wives—obsequious and coy in the presence of their men. Their voices were ever respectful, begging, it seemed, for forgiveness of their womanhood. Independent and fearless away from their men, in the presence of husbands they made themselves small and unobtrusive. While Nike bowed to and addressed Tope's male friends as "brother," as custom required, it was without the convincing ring of acquiescence that shuddered through the other women's voices. She was elusive and simply would not be touched by the demands of others. Her face told the world "I belong to me." Tope was unassuming and so generous that he was ridiculed by the others and even by Femi. Tope, a man born to be a husband, had married a woman who could never be a wife.

Within three months of her arrival, and a mere two weeks after the formal wedding, Nike was pregnant. She ballooned and her legs and arms swelled, filling with fluid. Moody and irritable much of the time, she refused to mask her discomfort behind long-suffering smiles. She was in labor for three difficult days and gave birth to twins.

The naming ceremony was held a week after the babies' birth. Tope's apartment was bursting with people, most dressed in formal Nigerian attire. I'd cornrowed my hair, and one of the women had made a Yoruba-style dress for me. Paper plates heaped with jollof rice, hot, peppery stew and bean cakes littered the room. I stood in a corner next to Femi. He held me tightly around the waist, gratified and pleased by my dress, my hair. I had begun to understand the Yoruba that rushed around me in a torrent, had picked up a few words and used them whenever I could.

The ceremony began with one of the older men acting as

priest, standing to address those gathered. He poured a libation, a sprinkling of gin, onto the carpet to honor ancestors still living in spirit. Turning to Nike and Tope, he spoke in Yoruba of their strength and love, together and separately, and the spiritual wealth the child would inherit from both families. He reminded us of the importance of the child to all gathered, of the stake we all shared in its future and our commitment to one another. Set on the coffee table were several bowls filled with ingredients symbolizing wishes for the child's life. Femi whispered in my ear the significance of each ingredient. "Honey so that life will be sweet. Water for the child to be great like the sea. Salt to know that life will be difficult." The minister dabbed a bit of each onto the tongues of the parents and child and the bowls were passed around the room for everyone to taste from and confirm the same blessing. Then the names of the children, Taiwo and Kehinde, were pronounced and the crowd repeated them as a litany. The sound swelled from a whisper to a chant. The close, cramped room smiled broadly upon these new members of the clan. Gifts of money were placed in a large bowl and presented to the parents.

When the babies were six months old Nike decided to go to school. She did well in night school, got a part-time secretarial job and soon bought her own car. Nike's independence sparked a loud and persistent chorus of disapproval from the others. More and more she and Tope fought, and at the end of each battle she threatened to leave him. Then, suddenly, the bitterness and the battles subsided. They began to live outside the shadows each cast, shaping a peace for which no one could guess how much they paid.

With their marriage a corpse disrobed of passion or concern, the others congratulated them on the silence emanating from their lives. The man who conducted the naming ceremony explained to me, "Where there is disharmony in one marriage, there will be disharmony in all. For we are wives and husbands together. Now that they have found themselves, my wife can respect me again."

"Why don't they just get a divorce?" I asked Sola.

Smiling cynically, he said, "Because we do not marry for happiness, my sister. We marry to seal our fate."

After a year at the publishing company, I learned that a local television station was looking for an associate producer and had a special interest in hiring a black. After lunch at a Greek restaurant with the station's personnel director, I had an interview with the executive producer for news and public affairs. I was shown into his office and waited for him for fifteen minutes. He was a tall, imposing man who strode forcefully into his office and appeared almost surprised to see me. Eyebrows raised in curiosity, he offhandedly asked, "Marita Golden, right?"

"Yes."

He had plopped his frame into the swivel chair behind his desk. His marvelously chiseled face alternated expressions. Then, twirling in the chair like a child, he pointed to a two-foot high stack of résumés on the corner of his desk. "Those are the applications for the position. I hope you're as good as Carol says. I really don't want to dig through that pile. Tell me about yourself," he demanded, settling back in the chair.

I told him about Columbia, the publishing company, my freelance writing. He seemed singularly unimpressed, and my throat grew dry, my voice changing register several times. His face was blank for a long while and then he asked, "How do you rate the magazine *Black Enterprise?*" The question appeared irrelevant and threw me. Regaining my composure, I said, "A good effort in a field too often neglected by the black press. They've got a ways to go, but with their budget and staff I think they do quite well. It's attractive and well written."

"And *Ebony?*"

I was warming to the game now and shook my head mockingly. "A tabloid promoting a black bourgeoisie dreamworld, only occasionally taking off the blinders to see the reality most blacks face."

He leaned forward, buzzed his secretary on the intercom and barked, "Susan, get me a subscription to *Black Enterprise.*" Standing up briskly and buttoning his jacket, he asked, "So when can you start?"

Taken back by the casualness of the offer, I stammered out an apology. "I'm going to spend a month and a half in Africa. I leave in three weeks." He was at the door, opening it.

"Well, write me from Africa. Stay in touch. The show starts in September. Our budget could be cut. But you've got the job." He went bustling down the hall. I trailed behind, trying to keep up. At the elevator he slapped me jovially on the back and smiled. "You're gonna be just great, kid."

Friday night. The seven o'clock news whispered from the television in a corner of the room. The dinner table was disheveled. We scanned each other's faces, comfortable, full of the meal and each other.

"Soon your African stew will be better than mine," he said, touching my hand.

"Your hamburgers will always be lousy," I chided. Then I brought his face close to mine with a long look of intent. "Let's live together. Soon you'll have your degree and we can get a place in the city." I lifted his plate, stacking it on top of a platter as I rose from the table. I gathered up the half-empty glasses, knives and forks, watching him from the corner of my eye. He sat thumbing through an enormous textbook on architectural design, his face worried, the book open before him where his plate had been. "Well, what do you think?" I demanded playfully, straining to regain my equilibrium.

"Let's wait until you come back." His eyes were riveted to the page before him.

"But why? What difference does it make?"

When he looked up, his eyes took me by the shoulders and shook me. "I want you to be sure."

"Of what?"

"Of what I have to offer. My life is too important to share with someone who can't understand it."

"Haven't I tried?"

"Of course. But having African friends and living in Africa are not the same. Go to Africa and then come back and tell me what you think."

"Femi, let's talk. We need to." I sat down again and as I did I felt him withdraw. He was finished. Not listening now. His eyes back on the page.

In the kitchen, as I placed the dishes in the sink, I dropped a cup on the floor, helplessly watching it shatter. Stooping to pick it up, I nicked my finger on a jagged piece of it. The energy I wanted to release in words had found expression in carelessness instead. Scrubbing the sink, I realized that I would never see him cry, admit to doubt or error. Say "I am sorry." But it was that strength I required to bolster my quicksand foundation. The revelations would come, I was sure, with time and my love, chipping away at and wearing down his defenses.

I had spent weeks reading articles and books on modern Africa, and grilling friends who had made the journey. I asked them everything. Now it was finally my turn.

To set foot on the continent that we no longer called home but that, in a historical sense, had birthed us, had become a necessary pilgrimage. A way of discovering who, indeed, we were. In the sixties Africa was a symbol and source of pride and regeneration. Renouncing the horrors of our slave past in America, we psychologically leapt past cotton fields and auction blocks back to the empires of Timbuktu and Mali, village life, Swahili, noble kings and tribal tongues. Hungrily we read, exchanged and discussed the books that revealed Africa's resilient cultures, its plunder at the hands of white conquerors, and its betrayal by its own sons. So those of us who became women and men in the late sixties sojourned to Africa in the seventies because peace of mind and self-definition required nothing less. The money I'd earned from free-lancing had bought my round trip ticket. Femi called me wonderful and brave. But I lived in fear of the unknown and frantically prepared for the future as though it were a final examination.

Again I looked at the unwashed kitchen curtains, grease-spotted, thick layers of dust frosting the fringes, and watched an army of cockroaches invade the sink I'd just scrubbed. A general disorder pervaded the apartment, making it appear heavy and uncomfortable. I wanted to clean its floors, walls, dress its windows in new, airy curtains. Put the mountain of papers on his desk in neat piles. Make order of his life. Bring substance to mine.

I wanted to make those rooms a place I would never want to leave. Suddenly I felt his hands at my waist, his lips against my neck. Having sensed my mood, he asked, "Would you like to go to a movie?" A peace offering. "Not really. I want to talk." I leaned against his chest, filled with questions and doubts his earlier charge had called forth. He turned me around to face him. "Why this endless analysis? I've told you what you must do. It's so simple."

"But, Femi, it's not."

A glance of harsh assessment burst like a flame in his eyes. I extinguished it by turning away. "So what movie do you want to see?" I asked gingerly, my hands trembling as I reached for the *Times* on the sofa.

10

As the plane descended into Kotoka International Airport in Accra, the land below astonished. Reached out with palm tree arms, nestled us against its red clay breast. Faces crammed the windows to drink in the replenishing view. We had left skyscrapers behind and now heard the earth's heartbeat welcome us home, caught the echo of a gentle laugh rippling inside the earth's skin. Laughter saved for our return.

The Trans-American charter flight was packed with lost-and-found cousins who had sprung from this soil. Who had played bid whist, snapped fingers to Aretha and talked, too eager to sleep throughout the eleven-hour journey from the night of New York to the promise of afternoon in Accra. The plane had almost touched down when somewhere in the front cabin a chorus of applause started and spread throughout the plane. While we clapped, others cried. I hugged the girl next to me. We knew this place. Remembered it. And as we applauded, we felt it tingle again inside our blood, like the name of a lover or friend silently summoned in moments of doubt.

"Look at all those black faces!" someone yelled, watching the ground crew scurry below us. Looking up, I saw what seemed to be thousands of Ghanaians standing on the balcony of the terminal. They held a banner that read "Welcome Afro-Americans." Standing outside on the ground, the land reached out again. It was the rainy season, and despite the hard, crystal gaze of the sun, the air clung, moist and heavy. Yet there was an openness, an absence of boundaries. I was certain that the ground on which I stood and the sky sheltering me from above would never end. Together they took my hand.

We were housed in dormitories at the University of Ghana, Legon, eight miles outside the capital city of Accra. Each of the tiny, close rooms had two beds, a table and a lamp. During the first days the halls echoed with complaints as the new wave of explorers settled in. One evening a rotund young woman—who, as the first person off the plane, fell dramatically to her knees, kissing the ground—burst into the room I shared with a girl from Philadelphia. "Can you believe this shit?" she asked, exasperated. "There's no toilet paper in the bathrooms." Extending her arms, she said, "And look at these damn mosquito bites. No wonder they call this place the white man's grave. I don't know about you two, but as for me, I'm checking into a hotel."

Accra was leisurely, unhurried. It basked in the sun, yawning occasionally to swat away a fly, smiling at itself in contentment. It had the atmosphere of a small southern town. Beneath my feet the earth was sunburned red clay. Palm trees were impressive sentries stationed along many streets. Hills, steep and dusty, seemed to surprise me at every turn. A good-natured haphazardness prevailed. Houses were at once fragile and solid, jutting out in no conceivable pattern onto main roads. And despite the hills the city seemed low, almost flat. When afternoon rains descended, black clouds rolled carpetlike across the pale blue sky and billowing white clouds. The rain, accompanied by thunder, darkened the sky and blanketed the city, while nature cleansed and rejuvenated us all.

My eyes became scalpels as I looked for the women to decipher their role, their place. They were everywhere, yet their presence was like a mist, intangible and fleeting. I saw them walking across the campus, down dirt roads, and along busy downtown streets, hawking oranges, bananas, or tomatoes from trays balanced on their heads. They were efficient and had a nononsense attitude while directing traffic, dressed in blue skirt, white blouse and a cap that made them look like WACs. The women who sold me cloth and souvenirs in the market were hard-nosed and gregarious, illiterate and shrewd. The air bustled with the rhythm of their voices, bargaining over each article as though lives hung in the balance. Their performance was raucous and endearing. I watched them, amazed. Coins and paper money bulged from the inside pockets of their wrappers. In the dank and musty government offices, where there was an air of stagnation, the women were girlish and coy, fingers painted, eyes dancing beneath layers of mascara. But wherever I found the women, purpose etched their faces; they were fueled by an energy I'd never seen in women at home. They hoisted heavy baskets of fruit or ground nuts into the back of mammy wagons, held down street corners from dawn to dusk, selling rice and pigs' feet wrapped in palm leaves, with a toddler playing in the dust, held to their breasts to feed, strapped to their backs to sleep.

Flagging one of the canary yellow taxis that zipped around the city, it stopped. "University of Ghana, Legon. How much?"

"One cedi fifty pesewas." Overcharged, I got in anyway. Settling against the backseat, I looked out the window at a panorama that was exotic and serene. "I won't let you be quiet in my taxi," the driver joked, turning to look at me. His dark face was crinkled by an impish grin. "What do you think of this place?"

"So far, I love it. Ghanaians are very friendly."

"We are your brothers. You American Negroes," he pronounced solemnly, making a sharp turn and gesturing with his right hand as he shrugged, "some of you come here and act in a disgraceful manner, but we know you were seized by the colonial powers and taken away to do their work. This is a concern of every Ghanaian." He paused and then resumed. "I want to go to America. How would I be received?"

"Well enough, but not as graciously as you receive others, I must admit." I mentioned that I was going to Nigeria and he laughed harshly. "You will not like them; they are bush people, those Nigerians. And Lagos, ha! You will smell it a mile before you reach it." When we stopped before the dormitory I paid him. He returned fifty pesewas to me, the amount I was overcharged. Waving to me as I entered the dormitory, he called out jovially, "Safe journey, my sister."

A student at the University of Ghana, Legon, Prince Wilson befriended me and two other girls with whom I'd been touring the city. Accra was dotted with discos alive and jumping day and night. One evening he took us dancing. The "Red Dress" was the size of a large living room, and its powerful sound system blared mostly American music. Al Green entreated, "Let's Stay Together" and Marvin Gaye begged, "Let's Get It On." Over drinks Prince promised to introduce us to his family. His father had three wives and eighteen children.

A few days later we met a friend of Prince's family, Mr. Jacobs, a retired civil servant in his late sixties.

Mr. Jacobs lived in Medina, a sprawling new township that felt and looked like a frontier. Entering the town we were greeted by what seemed miles of bushes, trees and foliage growing rampant, yet to be cleared. This landscape was dotted by an occasional house. All the dwellings were separated by at least a quarter mile. Some were ramshackle, hopeless efforts that could provide nothing more than mere shelter. Others were solidly built, with large porches, neat yards and cars parked before them. Tiny kiosks manned by undernourished women or small children were more frequent, offering the staple in-transit refreshment, Coca-Cola and hard, stale crackers.

In a few years the government hoped this area would be a well-populated suburb. But then there was no electricity, so at night a profusion of kerosene lamps became stars shining in windows, eyes swinging in the hands of children running evening errands.

Mr. Jacobs' uncompleted house rested on several cement blocks. The foundation of an additional wing awaited completion. A length of cloth hung across the front entry where one day a door would stand. Inside, the living room was intimate, radiating—despite its unpretentious furniture—a feeling of warmth and welcome. Dog-eared recent copies of *Newsweek* and *West Africa* magazine lay on the coffee table. Books lined the shelves of one entire wall.

Born to Ghanaian parents in Nigeria, at the age of eight Jacobs returned with his family to Ghana to live. Widely traveled throughout West Africa, he acknowledged both Ghana and Nigeria as home. Eagerly he grilled us about America, Nixon and Watergate, and invited us to return for dinner the next evening.

The next day, the others were not interested. They had bought a supply of strong, native marijuana and sat in the dormitory, giddy, eating mangoes and bananas. "But he invited us back," I pleaded.

"So what?" Sandra jeered, taking a long drag on the cigarette, closing her eyes and snorting deeply.

"Yeah, you go on, be our ambassador," Karen said lazily, gazing at me with only mild interest from her cot. I slammed out of the room, angered by their insolence, wondering why they were not as curious, as amazed by all we had seen as I.

"What of your sisters?" Mr. Jacobs asked when Prince and I entered.

"They didn't get back from Accra in time," I lied, self-consciously avoiding his eyes.

"I am sorry," he said, shaking his head, perplexed, as he ushered us to two chairs across from him. In the kitchen his wife and four daughters prepared the meal, gliding into the living room noiselessly to set before us fried bananas, ground nuts and large bottles of beer as appetizers. A chicken strutted into the living room, his head bouncing in spasms as he assessed and then dismissed me. The rhythmic thud of yams being pounded into a dish called foo-foo in a wooden mortar sailed into the room reassuringly. As I saw in other homes, Mr. Jacobs' wife seemed banished to the kitchen while he hosted the foreign guest. I was

frustrated by my inability to meet these women. For I knew instinctively they were the foundation on which the society rested.
I knew, too, that they could unlock the culture's real secrets for
me, but I also feared guessing what their status might portend
for me.

Mr. Jacobs' face had the same boldness engraved on the faces
of Nigerians. Yet it was softened by a mixture of wonder and patience that shone in the look of all the Ghanaians I had seen.
Behind thick-rimmed glasses his eyes danced in jest or wonder
pierced with intelligence. He entertained us with anecdotes and
cryptic criticisms of his fellow Ghanaians.

"What was it like under Nkrumah?" I asked.

He paused, toyed with the ground nuts in his palm and said,
"To quote Dickens, 'It was the best of times, it was the worst of
times.' He built monuments and office buildings. Gave us something to believe in. We thought, in the beginning, he wanted us
to believe in ourselves. But then we realized he wanted us
merely and only to believe in him. The way one believes in a
god." He shook his head sadly. "Anyone who did not support
him was thrown in jail."

"But what happened? I read his books; the theories seemed
perfect for Africa."

"The theories were perfect. The man wasn't."

"And his overthrow. Who was responsible? The CIA? The
Army alone?"

"It does not matter, for the first statue of himself he ordered
erected was the first nail in his coffin."

I asked him about Nigeria and Ghana and repeated the warning of the taxi driver. "You will hear such foolishness from the
mouths of Ghanaians. For many years Nigerians had settled
here. They are an aggressive, industrious people, no matter the
tribe. So, being more eager than we, they soon controlled crucial
areas of our economy. We were furious and so we rounded them
up and drove them out. While we slept, they worked. And most
of us will never forgive them that." He poured more beer into his
glass and concluded, "The problem is, we are still asleep."

His daughters brought out the meal—ground nut stew with
chicken and a huge mound of foo-foo, thick and gooey. I dipped

tiny balls of it into the stew and gulped it down. After a few minutes of watching my laborious progress, Mr. Jacobs laughed, "You have done well. At least you tried. Leave the rest if you wish." After dinner I met his daughters, each one tall, with neatly braided hair. Each one a replica of him. They were demure and awkward before me, even as they plied me with questions about America, where they hoped to study someday.

The black faces I had seen became a reflection. And despite tribal markings, because of lips and hue each face gave an answer I had searched for unknowingly all my life. And each face echoed my father's stories. Told me they were real.

Prince borrowed his brother's car and took me on a tour of some nearby towns and cities. We drove along rough, boulder-studded dirt roads and short, intermittent stretches of highway to Takoradi, a seaport town 118 miles from Accra. There I met Prince's friends, who were naval officers. We spent a weekend on their ship and driving around the sprawling, hilly town. In the daytime the town was sunlit and beaming. At night its breath was a whisper. The same languorous air of serenity that prevailed in Accra squatted over everything here. To my uninitiated eyes the poverty seemed quaint, almost benign. It lived in wooden shacks instead of cement projects. Gratefully, I witnessed no poverty of the spirit. Like Accra, Takoradi seemed suspended in time, halfway between past and present. The rains routinely washed away the inferior cement used to lay down the town's few real roads. Incongruously, a crippled 1968 Cadillac rested on bare axles before a sign advertising the skills of a native doctor.

From Takoradi we went to Kumasi, the homeland of the Ashanti tribe. I met the Asanta Heini, the spiritual leader of the Ashanti people. He sat bare-chested inside his whitewashed palace, a richly textured wrapper draping him from the waist down, several strands of cowrie beads bulging around his neck. He appeared more relic than royalty, nodding with disinterest at the tourists who bowed before his throne.

Cape Coast nestled against the coast of the Atlantic Ocean. Palm trees broke the high winds coming in off the water onto the pearly white sand of the beach. And it was there that we toured the Cape Coast Castle. Though the structure, seized by the British from the Swedes in 1664, was weatherbeaten, it was still formidable. In the main yard the cannons and walls used to turn back Portuguese, Spanish and German assaults still stood, lined up in perfect order as if awaiting imminent use. Miraculously, the clock in the tower still gave the correct time. The tour guide, wearing a tie-dyed dashiki, had moonlike eyes and a sonorous voice that echoed ominously as we walked through the dark, eerie castle. "Thirteen rooms made up the dungeon," he told us. "There were thirty-six such castles along the coast, with this and Elmira Castle being the largest. Three hundred people would be in a room at any given time." He pointed to the corners. "Pans were kept there for the slaves to urinate. Local slaves were trained to eavesdrop into the rooms to hear escape plots. Rebellious slaves were killed and thrown into the sea."

It was the last tour of the day and Prince and I were the only visitors. The dungeons sloped slightly beneath a murky, relentless darkness. The skin of the walls was as craggy and as black, I imagined, as the bodies of the people it imprisoned. Light entered through slits carved near the room's ceiling. It did not illuminate but instead cast shadows that lurked in every corner. I heard the tour guide's voice, hypnotic and frightening in its calm unraveling of the awful history of the place. But soon his voice receded, and as Prince and I followed him, curving and winding through narrow rooms into open, pitlike caves, I heard only and finally shouts of agony, screams, the clinking of chains. I smelled death and I looked at my sandaled feet and saw blood rippling across the floor's rugged face.

The sky was dark and cloud-filled as we came out of the castle. Vultures swirled in a brooding pattern overhead.

Driving back to Accra, I was mute, pensive.

"You are sad?" Prince asked quietly.

"Yes. I had read the books about it. But until today I couldn't realize how it really was."

"Not many of the Afro-Americans come this far into the country, you know. They do not want to see this monument."

"Perhaps it's just as well."

"Do you think so?" he asked, surprised.

"Many would feel betrayed by Africa. Would love her even less."

"Is that *your* feeling?"

"No."

I amused him. The wind was coming up furious now, off the water and into the town of rocks and hills. The sea smashed against the shoreline, tortured and angry, matching the emotions I felt inside. Through the window I watched the palm trees writhe and seem almost to break in the wind's grasp.

"And you don't hate them?" I asked Prince.

"Who?"

"The whites."

"Perhaps if they lived among us," he shrugged. "We could learn enough of their ways to master that impulse. But they have left us alone. We are no longer worthy of their exploitation nor even their contempt. And, my sister, for that we thank our gods."

On my last day in Ghana I spent the afternoon at the AEE Easy Eatin, a restaurant owned by a black American, James Elliot, from Chicago. Inspired by a pre-Black Power sense of Pan-Africanism, he had migrated to Ghana fifteen years earlier "because of Nkrumah," he told me, as though that explained everything. The specialty of the restaurant was soul food and it was a favorite haunt of young Ghanaians who were showing Americans the sights of Accra, or who merely wanted to be around black Americans. Elliot had married a Twi woman and was the father of two sons.

I sat in the courtyard eating fried chicken and potato salad, talking with a friend of Elliot's, another American named Calvin Burson. He'd lived in Ghana twelve years. He, too, had married a Ghanaian woman, and his daughter, a beautiful doe-eyed girl, sat on his knee. "Why do you stay?" I asked.

"Because it is where I want to be. In Detroit I was driving a taxicab and a friend of mine invited me to come with him on this trip to Africa to check out business prospects. So I bought a ticket, came with him, and we've been here ever since. We own a construction company that handles small projects, like schools and factories, for the government."

"Are you rich?"

"Far from it. But it's mine. I could never have done something like this in the States." He mashed his cigarette out and shifted his daughter to the other knee. "And, best of all, I don't have to deal with Charlie."

"Do you speak the language?"

"A little Twi, a bit of Ewe. I've been too lazy to learn."

"Have you been accepted?"

"Yes and no. I'm still an American. There's no way I'll never be that. And because of that, there are parts of the culture that I simply can't penetrate."

"What don't you like?"

"The tribalism. It's as bad as racism at home. And it's in everything they do, think, feel. Their loyalty is to family first, then village, and Ghana last."

"You sound bitter," I observed.

"I guess in a way I am. I know I've lost some of my idealism. I've been here too long. Seen too much. Twi against Ewe against Tiv—and me, I'm in the middle of it all."

"Sometimes the middle is a good place to be. You can be protected." I laughed.

"You can also be crushed."

"But you'll stay?"

"Yes. I've a family and, besides, I wouldn't know how to act back in my hometown in Alabama anymore. I'd be lynched or simply kill the first honkie that didn't call me mister. James tells me this is your last day in Ghana. Where to from here?"

"Nigeria. My boyfriend's from there, so I'll hook up with some of his people."

"Make sure he doesn't already have a wife."

"I already have," I said defensively.

"I know, but check some more while you're there. They won't tell you, but just keep your eyes open."

"Does that happen often?"

"You better believe it. I'm not trying to scare you. I just want to give you some advance knowledge that could help."

"Thanks," I said dryly, pushing my half-full plate aside, my appetite suddenly gone.

Elliot bustled over to our table. "Hey, Calvin, she tell you she's going to Nigeria? I warned her about Lagos. Remember the time we tried to import some building materials from Apapa port?" He shook his hand as though it had been burned, contorted his face, hunched his shoulders and screamed in a James Brown shout, "CONFUUUUUUSIONNNNNNNN." "Sister, if you want to see chaos and CONFUUUUUUSIONNNNNNNN, you just go on over to Lagos. You'll be back in Accra the same day." He laughed heartily, holding his stomach, his bulk shaking crazily.

"I'm a very determined woman," I said seriously.

He winked at Calvin and said gravely, "Okay, in that case I'll give you three days."

Once in Lagos, there was no mistaking it. My senses were immediately pummeled by a vicious onslaught of noise and movement. The traffic, stuck in a perpetual "go-slow," was a headless monster winding its way through the city. Taxis, Mercedes Benzes, motorcycles, Volkswagen buses, bicycles and people jammed the roads, many of which were mere stretches of dirt being turned into expressways by ruddy, sunbaked Germans and Italians barking orders at black workers digging trenches and hauling cement blocks. I had come from Ghana by road, chartering a Peugeot with five other passengers. Once in Lagos, we spent two hours driving to the taxi and bus depot at Yaba. Along the road barefoot girls in dirt-stained wrappers hawked oranges, canned milk and plantains to occupants of the stalled cars, their livelihood thriving on the stalled traffic. Eager young boys with sweat-drenched faces wove bicycles between cars, selling ice cream, cold milk and copies of the *Daily Times*. The thirst, frustration and fatigue of the drivers fueled their industry as well. We stood at a traffic circle for fifteen minutes. Up ahead a policeman directed the traffic brusquely, his face a stern, officious mask parodying authority. Like a doll wound up and out of control, he arbitrarily motioned some cars forward, holding others back with a threatening wave of a white-gloved hand. White gloves in such murderous heat. The traffic jam he created resembled a massive jigsaw puzzle, its pieces scattered by a petulant child in mindless disarray.

Femi's brother Jide had traveled to Germany, sent there by the government ministry for which he worked, for a six-month course of study. His wife, Bisi, did not merely welcome me but ushered me into her life. For the first few days I simply watched her life unfold, trying to gain my bearings in the city, which had the capacity to arm wrestle me to the ground.

One afternoon her younger brother arrived from his boarding school in Ibadan, distraught at having failed a crucial examination. She listened to his tale of anguish and defeat. Sympathy was offered with just the right mixture of stern criticism and encouragement, along with a small gift of money. A neighbor who had lost her last three babies, each within a month of their birth, and was now watching her six-month-old son battle an infection caused by ignorance and unsanitary conditions, spent an afternoon talking with Bisi. She left, her face less drawn and befuddled. Graciously Bisi introduced me to guests, and when the conversation turned to Yoruba, she firmly drew me into its web with a translation into English.

Mornings she coaxed and sometimes wrestled work out of her adolescent house girl, Iyabo. As the girl fried eggs, Bisi bounded into the kitchen, verbally pummeling her with a string of Yoruba/English abuses to hasten her work. Yet later in the day I saw her give the girl one of her old wrappers. Swirling like a whirlwind through the house, she bathed her children, Yemi and Olu, dressing them for school in starched white uniforms. Late morning I watched squeamishly as she casually wrung the neck of a live chicken, its body flapping in useless protest, plucked its feathers and made from it a stew. Noontime. Bisi and Iyabo pound yams for the afternoon meal. With two thick wooden pounders nearly as tall as they, wrappers pulled up tightly at their waists, bare feet planted on the kitchen's cement floor, sweat from their brow meeting the steam rising from the hot yams, she and Iyabo beat the yams inside a wooden mortar to a rubbery consistency.

Afternoons she insisted I accompany her on shopping trips to the nearby outdoor market, an open space dotted with wooden stalls laden with a profusion of fruits and vegetables. One long stall was devoted to the meat sellers—all men—who hovered over the chunks of beef that were turning brown beneath a fierce cloud of flies. Some women napped in the cool inner regions of their stalls, oblivious to the sounds around them. Children, some with horribly protruding stomachs, others bright-eyed and watching me curiously, played in the parched, dusty ground. I watched with amazement Bisi's subtle interplay with the traders. The women she haggled with over the price of okra and peppers were, in a sense, women she had known all her life. The dress she wore told them she had been abroad—and they would charge her more because of that—still, growing up she saw these women every day. She remained in touch with their thoughts and everything they wanted and dreamed of. Her European-style dress hardly obscured that fact that she had the same desires. Some market women wore only a bra above their wrappers. Others were old and toothless, their hair a design of tiny gray braids. A group of children hurled the surprised, mocking chant at me, "oyingbo, oyingbo," "foreigner, foreigner." I felt stripped, naked as *everyone*, it seemed, turned to stare. Bisi swiftly challenged the young culprits, pointing to the color of their skin and mine.

At night her sleep was interrupted because water only ran through the pipes after midnight. At 1 A.M. she awakened Dayo, her younger sister, and Iyabo, both sleeping on straw mats on the floor of the room we shared, enlisting their aid to collect water. The three of them filled huge drums with water, collected in the bathtub, to use for cooking, bathing and drinking the next day.

One night, while Iyabo prepared dinner, we rested in the living room, drinking Cokes. Bisi went into her bedroom and returned with a photo album. "Come, let me show you my family." She motioned for me to sit beside her. The first picture was of her as a bride ten years earlier. Dressed in a long, form-fitting white gown of intricately woven lace, she held a bouquet as she stepped out of a car. In the picture she was soft and youthful. Her face angelic. "You see, I wasn't always fat," she chuckled, pointing to her tiny waist in the picture.

"You were beautiful. You really were." I marveled. I looked at her face and saw that the softness and youth had dissolved into strength. Patting her stomach, which now resembled a beer belly, she sighed, "Too many babies. Too much marriage. Eight years in Britain. I went there to join Jide while he studied."

"What did you do in England?"

"I worked as a secretary and gave Jide my paycheck at the end of the week. Out of it he gave me money to run the house." She shook her head in disbelief at the thought. As she turned the pages I looked around the room at the crates of soda and beer, the stacks of material, and heard the chirp of the baby chicks she bred in the backyard—all for sale. All representing her livelihood in a society where women were required to work for survival and self-esteem. Gazing pensively at a photo of her two younger brothers and sisters, she said, "My older brother died last year and now the burden is on me. I must help support my own children and pay for the school fees of my sister and brothers. Soon I will have a stall in the market and will be able to do my duty then, as I should."

Suddenly I was awash with thoughts of family. Bisi's fierce allegiance to hers, Femi's to his. I had come to Africa, in part, to penetrate that bedrock. Now I wondered if I could.

"What is wrong?" she asked, touching my hand gently. "Your hands are cold."

"Does Femi have a wife?" I blurted.

Her hands still enfolded mine and her face was calm, unsurprised. "What did he tell you?"

"That once he had sent for someone, but it didn't work out."

"And you don't believe him?"

"I found letters addressed to him. Letters from a woman with his last name. Letters that began, 'My dear husband—' He never really told me what happened."

"That is uncle. He would not. Even we do not know what happened. The girl was to join him in America. Everything had been arranged and then suddenly the letters from him stopped. Jide and the girl, even her mother wrote, begging uncle for some reply, some explanation. But none came. It has been over a year since he wrote her."

"I met him fourteen months ago."

"Then it was you. Can't you see that it was you he wanted?"

"But why not write her? Tell her? How could he be so cruel?"

"That is uncle's way, and since it is you he wanted, that is not your concern."

One evening we visited Femi's uncle, "the Chief." Lagos at dusk is as frenzied as under the afternoon sun. Its pulse ever quickened, it is a city that bulldozes and sashays. At the crowded bus stop a short distance from Bisi's house we boarded a Volkswagen van, dubbed in the Yoruba vernacular *"kia kia,"* or quick quick bus. The drivers were notorious for plunging onto sidewalks or taking circuitous back roads to get through the "go-slow." A boy of about twelve, barefoot, dressed in a grimy, tattered shirt and pants, his feet caked with dirt, called, "Yaba. Yaba. Yaba." Instantly the motionless crowd activated, becoming a horde as everyone—market women laden with baskets of produce, uniformed schoolgirls, civil servants protectively clutching briefcases—scrambled for the bus. Bisi grabbed my hand, plowed through the crowd and boosted me into the van, squirming in after me. Inside it was hot and airless, the faces tense and preoccupied.

The Chief, one of the wealthiest men in the country, inhabited a palatial two-story house in a section of Lagos called Suru-Lere. The structure, imposing and forbidding like its owner, was conspicuous, squatting on the side of a dirt road lined with ramshackle wooden stalls from which women sold provisions and men sat on stools, sewing shirts beneath signs reading FAITH TAILORING—LONDON TRAINED. Ten feet from the main road girls bathed younger brothers and sisters, the children's naked brown bodies squirming as cups of water from a nearby metal bucket rinsed their backs and arms, soaped by a straw sponge. Boys wearing bell-bottomed slacks, platform shoes and sunglasses hawked SONY cassette players, transistor radios, tape recorders—all spread proudly on quickly thrown together display stands. The street was a metaphor for Lagos itself—restless, haphazard and impolite.

Behind ornately designed iron gates the compound of the house held two garages in which were parked a gleaming cream-colored Cadillac, a sky blue Mercedes, a cranberry-colored Datsun and a navy blue Volvo. A dozen robed and turbaned Hausa watchmen sat immediately behind the gates guarding against intruders. It was a house of low ceilings and long rooms decorated in plush green carpeting, solid, heavy chairs and sofas, and color photographs of the Chief and his children in formal African attire.

The steward led us upstairs, where the Chief sat on his balcony.

"*Ekuale,* sir," Bisi said, falling on both knees as a sign of respect.

"*Ekabo, Iyawo*" ("Welcome, wife"). He motioned us toward chairs next to him. Bearlike, with an inscrutable face, even informally dressed as he was, his bedroom slippers stationed beside his chair, the man was cloaked in the piety of his wealth. Bisi rose from the floor and timidly I followed.

"This is Femi's girl friend. She is visiting from America."

He acknowledged me with a short nod and then turned back to Bisi. "Have you heard from Jide?"

"Yes, sir."

"And how is he?"

"Ready to come home."

Then the conversation turned to Yoruba, became less tentative, more animated. Some of it I could decipher; the talk was of relatives, family obligations and the Chief's last trip to London. The steward appeared, shuffling in the doorway, barefoot in a wrinkled khaki uniform.

"Master, Chief Akinrinade is here."

"Tell him I'm coming. Matthew, did I get a call from London this afternoon?" The Chief asked impatiently.

Cringing beneath the Chief's hard stare, Matthew grinned sheepishly and scratched his head. "Oh, yes sir. Yes, *oga* sir. It was at two o'clock, I think. Mr. Wentworth."

"Did you take the message?" Matthew fumbled in his pockets, his face befuddled and concerned. "Well, where is it?" The Chief shouted.

"Don't worry *oga* sir. I go find am." And Matthew bowed, backing obsequiously out of the room.

"Matthew!"

"Yes, sir?" he asked innocently, scurrying back onto the balcony.

"What was the message?"

The odor of liquor rushed into the air each time Matthew opened his mouth. "*Oga* sir, I no *sabe* (understand)," he sighed heavily in Pidgin English.

"Get out!" The Chief exploded.

"I go find am. I go find am quick quick," Matthew said, hurrying away.

As we left, tiptoeing down the carpeted staircases, Bisi squeezed my arm, whispering, "The Chief is the one all the Ajayis fear and wish they could be."

One afternoon Bisi took me to Lagos Island. Lagos properly referred to both the island, which was the commercial nerve center, and the mainland, which was largely residential. Looking out the window of the taxi as we crossed the Carter Bridge that day, I spied a line of ships settled in the wharf below; still farther ahead I saw skyscrapers outlined craggily against the afternoon sky. The sight of the ships and tall buildings symbolized a dynamism I had not sensed in Ghana. Lagos was a boomtown, bustling and self-important. Hurried and brusque. Never mind the destination. The journey was all that mattered. Still, this potentially deadly rhythm touched my own restless soul. I was there because, like everyone else, I was an explorer looking for the end of my personal rainbow.

Tinubu Square was Forty-second Street without the neon lights. A ring of office buildings hovered over the square, which consisted of countless tiny side streets where everything, from shoes to Japanese color televisions, were sold. The stalls were humble on the outside, but once you responded to the sellers' enticing call, "Customer, customer," and entered the inner regions, a profusion of material goods awaited your choice. The tiny shops were stuffed nearly to bursting with jewelry, cosmetics, cloth, underwear, ladies' dresses, *galaes*, men's shirts, handbags, children's clothes, stockings, ties, pens, wallets and towels. And outside in the square itself one-legged beggars hobbled through the crowd of cars and people that teemed night and day. Pickpockets jostled the unsuspecting and gathered in clusters like birds of prey at each bus stop. Businessmen, pseudo and real, wearing three-piece suits or flowing native robes, drove Mercedes or were chauffeured in an Audi. Honda and Suzuki motorcycles zipped through the traffic, annoying and shaming the driver of the Peugeot with their mobility. Uniformed schoolboys in white shirts and shorts shouted curses at reckless truck drivers. Hausas from the northern part of the country squatted before an array of ivory bracelets, leather bags and cheap trinkets placed on a cloth on the ground. I stopped before one Hausa and he smiled, spotting my foreignness instantly saying, "Ah, soul sister, bring money, bring money." And the theme song for this extravaganza was the music of Earth, Wind & Fire blaring from a record shop, mingled with the satin sound of Nigeria's own Sunny Ade, his electric guitar drilling the air. An irritable symphony of car horns provided a reprise.

Lagos is an aggressively masculine city, and its men exude a dogmatic confidence. Though enterprising and diligent in public life, whose shape is determined by men, the women surrendered a large measure of their dynamism willingly, as if relieved of a burden. The men smiled from billboards advertising Star beer, ruthlessly maneuvered cars through traffic, leisurely waited on customers in the post office, strode along the streets in their green army uniforms. The intensity of their kinship was startling. Belligerently patriarchal, the men assumed their worth and waited indifferently for the women to prove theirs. I gathered the essence of this equation so vividly from all I saw that I knew on some level it was true. Yet it was this masculinity that made the men so undeniably attractive. Their self-consciousness translated into a roughhewn charm. Watching their deft, often obvious interplay, I understood why Femi gained my loyalty and why, if what I was told was true, so many black women followed these men back home. Nigeria was their country to destroy or save. That knowledge made them stride and preen in self-appreciation. This assurance became for an Afro-American woman a gaily wrapped gift to be opened anew every day.

Femi's cousin Sola advised me that once in Lagos I should look up an American girl married to one of his friends. Her name was Sara Bankole and we had lunch one afternoon at the Ikoyi Hotel. Foreign businessmen and tourists claimed the hotel's foyer and browsed at its newsstand stocked with international newspapers and magazines. I waited for her in the dining room while sipping a Chapman, a cold, fruity drink more sugar than alcohol. I had been gazing around the room, sizing up the people at each table, when I felt rather than saw her standing beside the table. Her face was open and secretive, animated and constantly unfolding into certainty and contradictions. I liked her immediately. Over lunch we traded personal histories. She was from Columbia, Missouri. When I smiled at the mention of Missouri, she grinned and said, "Yes, honey, there's black folk west of Harlem." She was the last of three daughters, doted on, overprotected, primed early to flee the stifling web of her parents' expectations. She confessed that her grades in high school were only average but good enough to get her into Cheyney State, a black college in Pennsylvania. With candor and a kind of reverse pride, she admitted going to college mainly "to get a husband," and in her junior year she found one. A twenty-five-year-old Nigerian student who planned to study dentistry. "The brothers wanted to take me to a motel. He wanted to get married," she explained. Loving him was an adventure. He was polite, generous and impressed her parents so much they forgave him for being foreign. They'd been married seven years and had three children.

She shook her head in amazement when I told her about Columbia, my writing, and the television job that waited for me on my return to New York City. "So tell me," I asked over dessert, "how is it to live here?"

"A lot of that has to do with who you think you are when you come. Whether you keep the culture and the people at a distance or try to come to terms with it all."

"But you're happy?" I asked eagerly, needing to hear this assurance.

"Yes. But that has nothing to do with the prospects for your success."

"That's not really what I wanted to hear," I said, stung by her honesty.

"But it's what you have to understand. I could tell you stories about women who've come and lasted three months. I could tell you ugly, bitter stories that would curdle the love I hear for your boyfriend every time you say his name. But I won't. I can't. Besides, if you took on New York City, Lagos will be a piece of cake."

She drove me back to Bisi's house, chattering steadily. But her warning had settled like a claw in my mind and I feigned a headache to camouflage the worry that gripped me. We exchanged addresses and promised to write. As I opened the car door, she touched my arm and said softly, "When you come back next year I'll do all I can to help you settle in. I promise you that. I can't make the settling in easier. But I can help you understand it." I hugged her earnestly and hard, beginning to compose in my head letters to her from New York. As I waved good-bye, her battered Volkswagen sputtering out of the driveway, her face became a map and I saw everything she had discovered in the three years she'd called Nigeria home.

From Lagos I journeyed to Ile-Ife, an ancient Yoruba town. The university around which the town was centered spread over many acres, its grounds dotted with ultramodern architecture. The town itself was parched, dusty and sleepy. Ibadan was a friendly city of steep hills and tin-roofed houses. From a balcony, one afternoon, the sloping roofs appeared to be steps leading to heaven. Ibadan bustled, but without the deadly fierceness of Lagos.

As the plane taking me back to New York pushed hard, irretrievably, into clouds, memories unraveled in my mind. I had snatched the shroud from the bowed head of my past. Now at night I would sleep fitfully, and a tribal marked face and the sound of a drum would haunt my waking hours until I returned.

In six weeks I had roamed from Accra to Takoradi, through Dahomey to Lagos. And as I explored this small portion of Africa, I passed through a jungle of startling, new, often wonderful emotions. A sense of community enveloped me during the journey. The tensions inbred by a society intent upon convincing me I did not exist had miraculously disappeared. No longer constrained to apologize for the accident of color, I'd felt free, for

the first time in my life, to become whatever *else* there was inside me, and I knew there was much more than a black woman
defined by white America. Sara's warning about the failure of
love transplanted to African soil had momentarily, but not per-
manently, stifled my optimism. For I loved Femi with the faith
of the true believer. My devotion was nothing more or less than
a crusade to regain the courage I needed simply to be. So I
swore that no matter what, Femi and I would not fail. We would
beat the odds. We had to.

11

After graduating from Cornell University, Femi moved to New York City. In my absence he found an apartment and got a job with an architectural firm, where he was one of several underpaid, overworked assistants. I moved in with him and within twenty-four hours the apartment glistened, neat and orderly. New curtains filtered sunlight through the windows, African batiks and masks scrawled messages across the walls. Plants hung from the ceilings flourished in corners. He surveyed the domesticity with pleasure, settled against it like a new chair that was already a friend. But as the months passed he grew increasingly frustrated at his job. He watched the sons of the firm's associates spend a few weeks with the firm and get assignments he was denied for lack of experience. And more than once he trained others, only to watch them be promoted to a position that was rightfully his. In bed at night, quivering with frustration, his large hand reaching for mine, Femi complained, "I must go home. To my country. Where I can be a man. I cannot do that here."

After dinner, he sat at his desk, precisely, patiently making blueprints, designing buildings he wanted more than anything else to see spring to life on his native soil. And increasingly he measured his worth in dollars and cents. As an associate producer for a nightly interview program, I performed a job that was stimulating and demanding. While researching and coordinating segments for the show, I met scholars, actors, celebrities and newsmakers. During a Broadway run of Steinbeck's *Of Mice and Men*, I interviewed James Earl Jones as background for a show devoted to a profile of him and his career. He was masculine, innocent, intellectual, and at odd moments an irrepressible clown. Though ostensibly we discussed his career, because of the breadth of his imagination and concerns we also touched on everything from his experiments with primal therapy to his image in the black press. I left his dressing room feeling hopelessly in love. And when the host, after listening to the two-hour tape of the interview, said jokingly, "Maybe *you* should do the interview instead of me," I answered with studied seriousness, "Maybe you're right."

Before one show Lord Snowden pulled me into a corner of the studio to discuss the upcoming interview. He was promoting a new book of photographs and had been doing television and radio promotional spots all day. On command the attractive blonde sent by his publisher to chaperone him slipped a silver goblet of champagne into his outstretched hand. "Now, Marita," he began, staring at me with an intimate gaze that cleared everyone else out of the studio. "Tell John that I will discuss the book and only the book." His face was lined and crow's-feet crinkled at the corners of his eyes, yet his was the most secure face I'd ever looked into. His arm around my shoulder, as though he was negotiating for a favor from a friend, he continued while sipping from the goblet, "I will not discuss the royal family, Princess Margaret or my personal life. Only my photography." His eyes appeared to plead for understanding. I assured him that the host was well aware of his desire. "Excellent. Excellent." He thanked me, drifting into the makeup room, pushing his reddish-brown hair back from his forehead. After the taping I had drinks with another associate producer on the show, and for a long time we talked about wealth and fame.

In the late fall the executive producer for news and public affairs assigned me to produce a special program. Two Swedish filmmakers had come to New York the previous summer and filmed a two-hour documentary on Harlem. The station now wanted to air it and I was asked to pull together a panel of blacks who would react to and discuss the film in a half-hour program following the show.

The film was a gripping, often brutal, sometimes ugly portrait of life in Harlem. It took a panoramic perspective of the community. The camera rambled over its landscape, focusing now on a minister and thirty-year resident of Harlem speaking of the changes he had witnessed, now on a jobless youth standing on the corner of 126th Street and Amsterdam Avenue, eloquent in his angry indictment of America. The voices of community activists, welfare recipients, middle-class homeowners, businessmen—all were heard. But the portion of the film that dealt with the prevalence of drug use was devastating. Scenes that appeared to have been staged showed junkies hovering in dark hallways injecting the poison into their veins with a skill sharpened by constant practice. The film showed a community at once struggling to survive and engaged in fierce patterns of self-destruction.

I sat in the darkened screening room watching the credits roll across the screen, stunned, trying to sort out my reactions. There was no doubt that the film was powerful. But I was disturbed by the lack of narration. The only voices heard were those of the people interviewed. What the film needed was a narrative to place the realities, shown so starkly, in an informed perspective. I wanted to hear words that would strip the film of its ability to merely reinforce the negative stereotypes that formed America's image of black urban life.

I discussed my apprehensions with the executive producer, who agreed, but he informed me that the filmmakers had gone back to Sweden and that it would be impossible to include a narration without their knowledge. I then suggested a foreword to the film that would achieve a similar end. He approved the idea. I contacted sociologist Joyce Ladner, writer Julius Lester, and James Turner, director of the Africana Research Center at Cornell University about sitting on the panel. All agreed, and Roger Wilkins, then a writer for the New York *Times*, agreed to host the panel.

A week after the panel was set, another black producer at the station, a longtime host of his own show, screened the film and vowed he would do everything he could to keep it off the air. Within days he'd sent out letters to local and national black leaders charging that the station was about to air a patently racist film. Soon the station was deluged with inquiries and protests. Turner and Ladner dropped off the panel. Julius Lester criticized the call to drop the film as a denial of free speech. The *Times* sent a reporter to the station who wrote a story about the controversy yet neglected to interview me. The executive producer then suggested that the film be screened by a cross section of the black community. Percy Sutton, then Manhattan's borough president, viewed the film with several members of the city's black political establishment and rejected the idea of showing it. A group of community activists and Harlem residents, however, watched it and demanded that it be shown. Florence Rice, a feisty fifty-four-year-old union activist and feminist, who was spokesperson for the group, sprang from her chair a moment after the lights went up and pointed a finger at me, saying, "You better make these people show it. That's Harlem, like it or not. Maybe if they see it, then we can get them to do something about it. I don't care what those downtown niggers say. They don't live in Harlem. We do." The twenty other people she'd brought with her broke into a rumbling, loud chorus of "Right on sistuh. You tell 'em."

But the station's executives took the low road and decided to postpone the film until the furor died. A year later the program was aired and largely ignored by the black and white media. Throughout the controversy I'd felt increasingly insecure as I assessed my future. The fratricidal nature of the station's internal politics disillusioned me. And after six months as an associate producer I felt as though I'd been locked in the trenches by enemy fire. Most of all, I felt like the proverbial spook by the door. Affirmative action had broken the latch. What, I wondered, would seal it shut again? I was writing less and just seeking, more often than not, to keep my spiritual head above water. I sought solace in yoga and meditation, took a fiction-writing course at N.Y.U. and began to write short stories. Soon I concluded with relief that my job represented a world I simply did not want. While continuing to perform my job as well as I knew how, I transferred my deepest loyalties to the life I would live when Femi and I returned to Nigeria. New York City had become strangely obstinate. On its streets I spied bloody footprints leading down blind, debris-filled alleys. I felt bludgeoned, betrayed by screeching, murderous subways and the growling aura of anonymity I'd once welcomed as a backdrop for the creation of my life. The mutterings of poets, preachers, bag women, bums —even my friends—curled into senseless mumblings. The city held a knife at my throat.

While I squirmed out of the city's hold, Wanda, my friend and compatriot, stretched it, cut it to shape. Working as a waitress, substitute teacher or receptionist to pay the rent between acting jobs, she had adjusted to the feast-or-famine nature of her career. Simultaneously she was awed by the spirit that was pushing me toward Africa to make/find a home and worried that in that world, which she had never seen and could not imagine, she might lose me forever. Sara and I kept in touch through a lively correspondence. At the end of one letter, in which she suggested items to bring with me or ship, she said, "Bring a house if you can."

Femi and I had become lovers, partners and friends. Our love was grounded in the sameness of our vision. Yet my dependence on him and his love was obvious and, for him, reassuring. I was as committed to returning to Nigeria as he—and for similar reasons. So it did not matter then that our interests and passions rarely seemed to converge, that he suffered through cocktails in East Side restaurants at my insistence, squirmed through Broadway plays and fell asleep at the movies. He was happiest, I knew, when he was working. Then I did not think Femi narrow or unimaginative. Instead, I congratulated myself for being loved by a man so devoted to achievement, so chronically ambitious.

I began to study Yoruba, going twice a week to the Olatunji Center for African Culture in Harlem. The effort buoyed me with a sense of purpose that enabled me to transcend the stranglehold of the city. And on Saturday afternoons I sat down for two hours of Yoruba conversation with Nike.

Three months before Femi was to return to Nigeria, his father died. He had lain ill, immobilized, for months, with the family in Nigeria, his children in the States, dreading, hoping against, anticipating his death. At seventy-four he left behind eight wives, thirty-two children and an estate over which the family would quarrel for years. The evening Tope came to tell us the news he and Femi huddled in a corner of the living room, their faces heavy and burdened. Immediately Femi retreated to the bedroom. Tope explained to me what was happening in Nigeria and described the thirty-day wake-keeping that would precede their father's burial. He spoke of the guilt he and Femi felt for being absent at this time of crisis. "Neither of us has any money that will help. So we can only send letters filled, instead, with advice and consolation."

Femi lay on his side facing the wall. The back I had touched so many times was a barrier, his whole body a warning sign. I sat beside him in silence, wondering about his father. Had he loved his father as I had loved mine? Had his father, who spent perhaps three nights a month with each wife, loved some children more than others? Was Femi petted or ignored? But even if he only saw him rarely, from afar, love had been ignited. The stony grief beside which I lay informed me of that. And so I touched him, his back unyielding, frozen beneath my touch. My hand traveled along his spine, offering a healing touch. The touch no one had blessed me with in my grief. The touch for which I had ached and of which I had dreamed in my mother's four-poster. Standing beside my father's grave. I curled beside him, needing no more than this connection, this act of faith.

"How can you think of *that* now?" He turned to look at me in disgust. "Don't you see I want to be left alone?"

"I just wanted to comfort you," I said, shaking my head in self-defense.

His response was a brusque shift closer to the wall. Blinking back tears, I rose from the bed and ran into the living room, where I slept that night on the sofa, fully clothed, restless, dreaming of his hands, which never came, retrieving me from solitude, placing me on the bed in the wrinkled curve my body had made.

Three months later Femi returned to Nigeria. I stayed behind in New York with the understanding that I would join him once he had gotten settled in a job. But after five months he had not found employment, and his letters, one after the other, urged me to wait in New York until he found work. Then one evening I wrote Femi a letter telling him the day and time I would arrive in Lagos. I loved him, I said in the letter, and the fact that he had yet to find work did not mean I loved him less. I wanted to be with him no matter what. So on September 13, 1975, I left J.F.K. International Airport with fifteen hundred dollars, my typewriter, five suitcases, and a bounty of faith in myself, Femi, and whatever waited for me on the other side of the world.

12

After two days of relatives and friends greeting and appraising me, Femi and I were alone. After we had spent six months apart, our glances met with the slow-kindling desire of interested strangers. I sat on his bed beneath a rolled up mosquito net. His face was hungry and mean as he paced the floor before me. Self-satisfied laughter wafted into the room from the parlor at the end of the hall; there his uncle, the Chief, entertained guests who sipped imported scotch and native palm wine. In voices that regularly commanded the attention of others, they measured the one-month-old military regime. The chant of Moslems praying at a nearby mosque rolled in waves through the night air.

Femi had lost weight, appearing thinner than I had ever known him. I feared asking why. My throat was parched, the muscles strained. I feasted on him instead, the sight of his body, remembering dreams that placed it beside me at night. In my

mind I delved into his presence, wondered why it had become a
skittish phantom. Beneath the bristling, invisible armor of anger
he was chastened and afraid. "Come sit beside me," I begged,
my voice cracking and unsure. "We have not talked or touched.
There are things we must say." I thought of the people at his
brother Jide's house, where I had spent the first two days, their
voices gay, tangled music churning around me.

Again I reached for him, this time with false nonchalance. "I
don't really believe I'm here. Convince me that I am." He looked
up, as if startled by my presence. His eyes were distant, had long
ago traveled past despair, and his words came like fists, striking
out at enemies imagined and real.

"I'm a stranger in my own country. Everything has changed.
Without money you might as well be dead. Even then no one
would care. I've yet to find a job. Either you must be British-
trained or belong to another tribe; otherwise the salaries are too
low. I did not go to America to come back to my country and
starve." The old arrogance throbbed in his last words, and for a
moment he stood with the composure he displayed the night we
met. But then he confessed, "I have had to borrow money from
my uncle, and nothing pains me more than that."

His letters to me in the States were scrawled, angry and
tense, charting his confusion and the steady unraveling of his
hopes. Taking them from my mailbox, the envelopes singed my
fingers as I imagined the words pent up inside. There were days
when I shuddered at the thought of slitting the seal, and instead
I buried the letter among a pile of bills.

"And when I returned to my town," he continued, "they all
asked, 'Where is your car?' Even my mother respects me less because I did not return plastered with paper money, bearing gifts
for them all. So I gave them my clothes. The shirts, the pants,
the shoes you bought me you will see on my brothers and
cousins." He collapsed onto the bed beside me. "Everything they
told us was a lie. Go abroad and study, when you return—"

I placed my fingers at his lips. "You think I will never know
your pain because I am a woman. I know it and I feel it because
I love you. Accept that as enough."

I kissed him, my lips groping with desire against his cheeks.

His hands possessively fingered my spine and I kissed the bridge of his nose, the entrenched bags beneath his eyes. His breath warmed my chin and my tongue navigated the outline of his lips. Inside his mouth it was moist and we met and his fingers pulled my panties down my thighs. Half clothed, awkward, on the edge of the bed we took one another, sliding to the carpeted floor with no time for orchestrated desire. We traveled fast, hard, resistance melting in our wake. We arrived, hearts bursting against our chests. Above me he panted, surprised and grateful, sweat from him drenching my neck.

Beneath the sheets we were quiet, relieved. The Chief's guests departed. The doors of their chauffeured cars closed hard, the night watchman opened the whining gates and the cars navigated the pockmarked road outside the house.

"And so you will understand why you must stay with Jide and Bisi," he said. "They have room for you. Your presence here is a reminder of my dependence on my uncle."

"But we should be together."

"We will be. Soon. And we will marry soon. Have patience, please." He sunk deeper into his pillow, drifting into repose and finally sleep. I did not sleep, for my thoughts danced crazily, hummed audibly at the edge of my brain. I had spent my life always becoming the woman men I loved needed me to be. Etching my shadow inside the curve of their love. Taking cues from the sound of their voice, the suggestion of a touch. Fatigued and overexcited, my will flexed inside me like a child turning somersaults in the womb. Slipping from the grasp of wakefulness, I tumbled into dream, where I was baptized by a contentment so cool and pure it opened my eyes. I whispered into the room's still, waiting darkness, "I will tame this adventure into a life."

Six weeks before my arrival in Nigeria, the eight-year-old military regime of Yakubu Gowon was toppled. While he attended a meeting of the Organization of African Unity (OAU) in Kampala, a cadre of senior army officers seized control of the government.

Gowon was named head of state in the tense months before the start of the Biafran civil war. Because he did not belong to any of the major tribes that traditionally jockeyed fiercely for power, he was seen as a pragmatic choice. For at that moment in Nigeria's history any attempt to appoint a Yoruba, Hausa, or Igbo leader would have merely plunged the nation even more bitterly into the drive toward self-destruction that had already become irreversible. The foreign press took to him and dubbed him a hero for navigating Nigeria through a brutal three-year civil war that quashed the forces of secession. When the war ended, Gowon promised a return to civilian rule. But the years of leadership had changed him; he wore the trappings of power as though born fully draped in them, felt himself a diplomat, scholar and statesman. Soon it was evident that he would not willingly step down. Simultaneously Nigeria began to boom and was gripped by an orgy of often ill-advised, ill-planned development. Huge oil revenues from the once rebellious Eastern region financed it all. But development did not mean schools, hospitals and low-income housing but rather expressways, bridges, gleaming office buildings designed and built by an invading army of European and American firms gorging themselves on the country's rapid growth. Nigeria soon resembled an adolescent battling the physical and emotional onslaught of puberty. Crime increased. The cities overflowed with migrants from the villages. In the rural areas farms were left fallow, forcing the government to import more food each year to feed nearly seventy-five million people. Corruption became audacious and in some quarters was even respected. The old values faced slaughter at the hands of imported styles of thinking and dress. And year after year the promise of civilian rule was denied.

A charismatic, stern Moslem officer headed the new regime. The priorities on his agenda were the routing out of corruption and the instilling of a sense of national pride in a country caught in a whirlwind of illusion and decay.

Femi's mother was the sixth wife of his father, and she gave the man three sons. Femi was the middle child, precariously holding down the center between an older brother, Jide, revered because he was the first, and Kunle, the youngest, spoiled because he came after ten years of barrenness. At seventeen Kunle was a bamboo shoot, sprouting gangly and thin, several inches taller than both his brothers. After graduating from high school, he left their hometown of Ado-Ekiti to come to Lagos to prepare for the college entrance tests. He badgered me with requests to bring him a pair of blue jeans when next I journey to the States, and his was the only voice that brushed against me, raw and hostile. He could not forgive his brother for loving a foreigner and I was bothered intensely that I cared.

Jide had Femi's face, but on him it was a puzzle. It was handsome, the lines that defined it chiseled deep. It was a face that was appealing, one that I could not predict, struggled to trust. Like the face of his brother, it was a mask. In the evening, when the tires of Jide's Peugeot crackled over the debris-filled road outside the house, Bisi marshaled their apartment into order and calm. The children Yemi and Olu, on the floor watching reruns of "Kung Fu" amid a symphony of laughter and complaint, were shushed. Her hand retrieved scattered clothing, objects, clutter, hiding them quickly. She had arrived in the house only moments before from her stall in the market, where she was now sending her house girl to pack the canned goods away and lock the doors for the night. Her glance scanned the table setting. Wringing her hands in anticipation, she tied her wrapper tighter at the waist, disappearing into the kitchen. When Jide entered the house, she came into the living room as though she had not left the house all day. "*Ekabo* ('Welcome') my dear," she said gently, with a look gauging his mood. He tossed a distracted "*Ekuale*" ("Good evening") at her and slumped into a chair as the children scrambled onto his lap. Bisi ran her home and business with demonlike efficiency. Yet Jide inherited total control over her life when he entered the house at ten minutes after five. The voice that barked—ordering the children to begin their homework, Iyabo to fry plantains—became a whimper. Jide often appeared indifferent, fatigued by the rituals of their union. And because his power was assumed by all, he rarely had to use it.

Like the other men I met, Jide watched me with covetousness and curiosity. Their words approached me on tiptoe and exempted me from a host of burdens placed on their women. I could not miss the threat, however, that they patiently gathered other expectations, perhaps even more exacting, to balance on my shoulders. For, looking at me they saw skyscrapers, spaceships and technicolor movies. I looked at them and saw a chance to reclaim a past that spat me out onto the shores of another world. We stumbled through these illusions to find one another. And reality had dug thick craters in that earth, poised inches away from each step.

"Sometimes I am afraid for uncle," Bisi said as she counted the cans of evaporated milk in the carton. Writing the total on a sheet of paper, she mused, "One day he will lose everything he wants most because of his pride."

"He hasn't told me everything, and I need to understand what's happened since he came back," I said.

Pushing the last carton into a corner of the room, she began, "When he came back, uncle was certain he would find a job very soon. He applied for jobs and expected the salaries one would earn in America. He turned down five positions because he thought the salaries were too low. When Jide came back from Britain it took months before he was employed. We reminded uncle of this and warned him not to throw away his chances. But he insisted something would come. He was hired for a job with an architectural engineering company a few weeks before you came, but the day before he was to begin he was told the position had been eliminated. Later he found out the owner had hired one of his brothers."

I recalled how little intimacy my pleas had won me. The persistence of my negotiations for revelation made him still tighter, ever more elusive. "I have loved Femi for two years. And each year it is the same. He doesn't tell me what he feels, and so he doesn't tell me the truth."

"Uncle will never tell you everything. Do you think Jide confides in me?" she asked, her voice shaking as though stung by the memory of an offense. "But uncle will share more with you because you are an American." I squelched the envy in her voice, saying, "I have yet to find the words that can defeat his silences.

"And the Chief," I asked, "why won't he help?"

"The Chief only helps his wives and children. He will donate money to build a church or a school, something that will bear his name, while his relatives go wanting."

"But what about the extended family?"

"It is the poor relations who extend themselves and their money. The rich ones expect and receive gifts from the others to honor their wealth, as though they were gods."

"But he has given Femi money."

"And the Chief will see that he never forgets the debt." Her voice softened. "Perhaps he did not tell you this because he could not. Because of the pain."

"I know that. I understand it. I just can't accept it."

Afternoon. The Chief's house was taciturn, waiting in patient repose like a satisfied wife for a husband's return. In the hallway the washman pressed the expensive, richly colored *sokoto* (pants) and *bubas* (shirts) the Chief wore with the majesty of a monarch. The clothes sat piled a foot high on a table beside the man. He worked quietly, attentively honoring his task. It was a house that had no woman to worry over it. The Chief was estranged from both his wives. Because the house had no mistress, beneath its presumptuous frame it slouched, careless and untidy. The steward, Matthew, spent most afternoons sleeping in a tiny room adjacent to the garage, or stationed at the gate talking to the Hausa watchmen. Their numbers ranged from a solitary Mohammed—the only one actually hired by the Chief, who resembled a barroom bouncer despite the beatitude of his face—to twenty or more friends and relations whom he fed and who slept with him at the gate at night, a silent, shifting horde.

Still, there was a grace inside the house, asleep beneath the dust Matthew never fully wiped away from mahogany liquor chests and bookcases; seeking refuge behind the yellow tint spreading like a fungus over the expensive chairs and heavy brocade curtains imported from London; and mangled inside the sound of the refrigerator clanking with age because no one remembered to call a repairman. But day after day the house was killing Femi. Stiff and formal with the Chief, he averted his eyes as he bowed in greeting and respect to him. The Chief was uninterested in us, untouched by our presence or by Femi's suffering. In the daytime Femi paced the large rooms, his energies bored children threatening to turn mean.

"Where have you been?" Femi asked as I surprised him on the balcony, where he was reading the *Daily Times* for what I imagined was the third time that day.

"I've found a job," I said.

"Where?"

"At a girls' school in Lagos. Jide drove me in this morning. I'll be teaching English and I start in two weeks."

"I'm glad for you," he said slowly, looking at his hands. Then, rousing himself, he laughed cynically, "But you are an American. You could be head of state." He moved to the banister, clutching it, and then gazed out at the road, over the tops of hibiscus trees flourishing in the front yard. Then he turned to me. "I called about a position this morning and told them I'd studied in the United States. The manager told me only British-trained architects had anything to offer. You go out and get a job with two American degrees." He shook his head sadly. "You make me ashamed of myself and my people."

"Don't ruin this for me. Don't ruin it for us," I pleaded.

Embarrassed, he sat down and asked, "How will you get into Lagos?"

"I'll go in with Sara in the mornings. She lives near Jide and works near the school."

"I went to the registry for the marriage license," he said. From his pocket he pulled a wad of tissue paper. Resting it in the palm of his hand, his fingers opened the paper to reveal a ring, a solitary, gleaming gold band. "I will buy you a better one than this when we are settled."

"But how—???"

"Jide gave me the money to buy it."

I reached for it and placed it on my finger. "It fits perfectly. When will we marry?"

"In a month's time."

Sara's house became a haven for me. It was cluttered, filled with the voices of her three children and open to an endless procession of drop-in visitors. There I practiced my Yoruba, marveled at the fluency of hers, ate fried chicken and apple pie, and listened to her gossip with neighbors. Automatically she became my mentor as well as my friend. She coped unperturbed with a three-day electricity blackout or a daylong loss of water. Sara was possessed of a caustic, never-wilting humor, sometimes tarnished by smugness. Her eyes scanned the tapestry of people and events around her and missed nothing. Her walk was part swagger, part muscle-flexing charge. On weekly trips to the markets she taught me by means of example how to bargain as ruthlessly as any Nigerian. Her husband Wole had established a lucrative private dental practice, and he was as subdued and modest as Sara was exuberant. Yet, despite her love for him she seemed ever on the prowl, by gesture and speech, for the attention of others. The Nigerian men adored her, for she acquiesced to the image of African womanhood while maintaining her Americanness. Bowing ostentatiously as a mock sign of respect to one of Wole's friends, just as a Yoruba woman would do, she rose and stabbed the man with a remark that drew blood, flirted, yielded herself up to him and denied him—all at the same time. But her substance beneath the shell was too hard, too aware to be anything other than an American woman. And it was that substance that mystified and attracted the Nigerian men. Awed, I watched her performance, took copious mental notes, but it would be years before I knew what it all meant.

"How has your marriage survived?" I asked her as I reached in the refrigerator for a Coke. The children were napping; her house girl washed clothes in the bathtub. The apartment was so quiet our voices nearly echoed.

"Because we're here, or just because?"

"Both."

"I don't know. I honestly never thought about why we've made it this long. I guess I've just been so content with the fact that we have, I never wondered why or how." She stopped and then said, "I know it's taken a lot of forgiving and forgetting from both of us." Her face settled into repose as she outlined the print on her Coke bottle, appearing unconcerned by her revelation and my probing.

"I can't believe how much, how fast I've changed in the few weeks I've been here," I mused. "It's like this has always been my life. I can't imagine ever wanting anyone else."

"You'll soon learn that in a real marriage 'someone else' can often make very little difference," she said slowly, measuring every corner of my face for the effect of her words.

"Why?"

"Our husbands will forgive infidelity. But a betrayal of our most important duties as wife, that's what they'll never forgive."

"But what duties do you mean?" I asked, lost in the maze of meanings her words subtly constructed.

"The duty to set the stage on which their lives unfold."

"Is that the only thing?"

"It's the thing that defines and forgives everything else."

"The contradictions of all this seem unbearable."

"You learn to live with them," she said, eyeing me skeptically as though my confession undermined some measure of her faith in me. "And after a while they don't bother you at all."

13

At 6 A.M. Ikorodu Road was a blackened canvas slit by an occasional headlight. In the darkness turning imperceptibly to light, the road roused itself, stretched its loins and felt its blood course. Thirty minutes more and a caravan of traffic snarled, twisted, stalled, would map every point on its body. Sara worked for an oil company a block away from the school I taught in, so we rode into Lagos together each morning. It was a two-hour drive that left us wilted and irritable as we finally reached the mainland. On her car radio the disc jockey, who read ads and the news but never gave the time or temperature, spun Bill Withers' "Lovely Day" at the top of each hour. We traveled from the fading remnants of night, through the startling sight of sunrise, to the sun becoming a hellish globe by eight o'clock. Alternate routes into Lagos from the surrounding areas barely existed, so everyone jammed the same thoroughfares. The first morning I witnessed the mass of cars I imagined that a coup or some national emergency was forcing the entire city to flee.

White-shirted civil servants turned murderous, racing the engines of Datsuns or Toyotas to move an inch ahead in the line of traffic. But Sara's tan arm tossed out the window, her biting yet innocent smile and her request in Yoruba, "*Ejo, oga, fun l'oja*" ("Please sir, give way") defeated the most stubborn driver and kept us most often at the front of the "go-slow."

The school was in Ikoyi, an affluent preserve inhabited by senior civil servants, foreign embassies and expatriate businessmen. Its roads were wide, twisting and miraculously paved. Houses that resembled estates lined each side of the road. Behind some gates stewards clipped lawns and drivers washed expensive cars. Grace and comfort tinged the air. Absent were the mountains of trash and garbage that were virtual signposts in other parts of the city. Assurance marked the stride of the Indian, English and American women who shopped in the boutiques and waited in the salons of the shopping centers erected to distract them from boredom and discontent.

The classrooms at the Lagos Comprehensive Girls' School were long, low-ceilinged, constructed of rough-edged cement. It was the dry season and the rooms trapped every blistering ray of sun. The floors were crumbling, large holes gaping beneath the crippled, scar-faced desks. On very hot days the odor from the toilet at the end of the hall became a sentry stationed at the door. The school, formerly private, was taken over by the government two years earlier. Once the school was highly rated for the performance of its students on the General Certificate of Education (GCE), ordinary (O)- and advanced (A)-level tests, the academic hurdles left as a legacy by the British. Now, however, its students performed poorly. Reflecting this degeneration, the compound looked neglected, with grass growing in thick clumps and the path to the main building constantly waterlogged.

The girls' faces, some blank with ignorance, others calm with knowing, strained with the effort to fathom an answer, hunched over the tops of thirty-five desks. The third formers sat writing an essay describing a favorite character from a novel or play. Inside the school uniform—purple, striped, sleeveless dresses—their adolescent bodies bloomed. Large breasts pushed against the front of some uniforms, threatening to spill out of the V neckline slit below the shoulderblades. The hips of some left creases at the backs of dresses, and their hands forever roamed to smooth the wrinkles over their behinds. Their hair was woven into a tapestry of braids, some twisted with dark string and shaped into elaborate cones, others cornrowed as simple and neat as a house girl's. They were effervescent and bright, chattering birdlike in the halls and the compound in Yoruba or Igbo, although English was officially required at all times. In class they spoke and wrote haltingly, with less certainty, a language that bore the imprint of British formal English, Pidgin English, their ethnic language, and slang picked up from imported American and Indian movies.

Their eyes conferred deference and respect upon me. And the same respect that required some of them to prostrate themselves before elders and parents had sapped a sharpness of intellect from them already. They endowed me with authority and wisdom. But there were questions they should have asked but never would. They would simply never imagine them.

I slipped easily into the task of teaching. For forty-five minutes four times a day I was listened to and watched. Pacing the cracked cement floor around the room, walking between their desks, I blew the dust from all the knowledge I had and offered it as a gift and a necessity. I chastised and stroked them. Both intimate and forbidding, I shared a bond with them based on memories of my sixteenth year—unsure, trembling, certain I was misunderstood. In return, they flocked to my desk at the end of class to gaze, smile and offer to carry my books for me back to the office.

From a classroom across the hall I heard shouts, yelps, the movement of chairs, and at regular intervals a muted whistle sound cut the air. Walking around the room to examine the girls' papers, I moved toward the door and looked into the neighboring classroom. The entire African history class was being punished. The girls squatted on their knees, ringing the walls of the room like a necklace. Mr. Idowu, short, intense, Napoleonic in bearing and self-conception, strode before them, twisting a long wooden pointing stick in his hands. "I will not tolerate unruliness in my class," he barked, casting a look along the line of girls that reduced them to rubble. "I cannot lecture in the midst of laughter and playing and note passing. The disease of disrespect will be cured, once and for all, or you will leave my class today." He constantly interrupted my paper grading in the office with soliloquies on Nigerian history. At the end of his speeches he would smile smugly and ask, "You didn't know that, did you?"

"You have tested me today and you will reap your reward," he told the girls. Dramatically he stopped in mid stride and turned, brandishing the pointing stick, which was positioned just below his waist. "Etta, come forward," he commanded. The girl, small, light-skinned, huddled against the student next to her, who with a loud laugh pushed her up from her knees and to the front of the room. Etta danced in fear before him, extending her palm, her face cast onto the floor. "Stand still," he shouted, and the words riveted her body. As she looked up from the floor, the cane landed on her palm. She hobbled away, rubbing her hand against her dress. "Margaret." The next girl, taller than he, strode forward, her teeth clenched, her large, manlike palm almost touching him. Idowu gathered energy like a pitcher perched on a mound and whacked the girl's hand furiously. She dropped her hand casually and spat out a final parting glance.

The line of girls was now raucous and rowdy. No longer a test of wills, the exercise had become burlesque. Each girl conquered him by mute indolence or submission to punishment, with fear genuine or feigned. For Idowu it did not matter, for he greeted each girl with a special look earned by her particular behavior, each look a mixture of contempt and longing. The bell rang and one of my students joined me in the hallway. "Should I collect the papers?" she asked.

"Yes. Yes, Catherine," I answered, my eyes still glued in horror to the charade. "Put them on my desk. I'm coming." As the last girl came forward, Mr. Idowu spotted me, and for a fleeting moment his tiny eyes were filled with the same passion and repulsion with which he stabbed the girls. I turned away, feeling as though I had looked through a keyhole, stumbled into a room that was assumed to be locked. I gathered my papers from my desk and hurried back to the office.

As I entered the office I saw Mrs. Ogunade, bulging in the sixth month of pregnancy, unfolding on the desk of Miss Chukwu a ream of cloth she was selling. Ingratiating and overbearing, Mrs. Ogunade went on and on about the beauty of the nondescript material. Miss Chukwu, a young Igbo woman, eyed her glacially, dismissing her with the assertion, "You know, I've just come back from Britain and I rarely wear native dress except on special occasions. And, besides, this is too common." Reminding her of the tribal difference that separated them, she said, "In the East we do not wear material of this type."

Mrs. Ogunade folded up the cloth wordlessly. Then she said, "Yes, Madam Britain. Perhaps you would be better to go back there."

Mr. Idowu entered the room, mopping sweat from his forehead with a rumpled handkerchief. He stood before my desk, immovable, demanding.

"You must be very tired, Mr. Idowu, after all the exercise you got in class today."

"Ah." A cheshire cat smile spread across his face. "I think you do not believe in corporal punishment?"

"No, I don't. I don't need it."

"Perhaps in your country. But trust me, you will need it here. If not today, in time."

"I gain the respect of my students through concern, not threats."

"Your idealism is refreshing. Isn't that an American trait?"

"And what of your cruelty? Is that African?" I shouted.

"Cruelty, you call it. Ask any of my students. They do not view it as such. They know it is called for. They expect it."

"But they mock the substance of it, so it has no effect."

"Just ask your students and you will see," he assured me, sliding confidently behind his desk.

The next day I assigned my fifth form class to write an essay either in favor of or against corporal punishment. That evening, as I graded the papers, I discovered that twenty-five out of thirty of the girls were in favor of its use.

14

Our wedding was modest. Bisi and Jide witnessed the officious, quick ceremony at the registry. Femi looked handsome in a cream-colored crepe suit I bought him one summer as a birthday gift. Bisi had dressed me in a pink and green *buba* (blouse) and *iro* (wrapper), with matching *galae* coiled around my head. Beneath the satiny embroidered material I felt regal. In my parents' house I was Marita Golden, molded like clay by the touch and warm breath of their legacy. In college I reached for a torch and added the postscript "black woman." Now, I wondered, in the house that one day would be Femi's and that would also be mine, who would I be? This quest, spurred by love, was just beginning. I had become an Ajayi. And as I said, "I do," promising, excited and relieved, to "love and honor" Femi, I was certain that an Ajayi was what I would always want to be.

In the car, driving back to Jide's house for the reception, Femi was subdued, apologetic. "When I have money, we will marry again," he said. "We will have a big, traditional wedding. Then all my family will come. The way it should be."

"That's not important to me," I assured him, piqued that in this moment of ultimate happiness for me he was still unsatisfied. That night we spent together at the Chief's house. "Now I will move here with you," I said.

"No, you can't," he insisted.

"But now I'm your wife."

"And it is because you are my wife that I want to give you more than a room in the home of my uncle."

We were in bed. Beneath the warm afternoon stillness of the nearly deserted house our bodies were ripe after love. Femi laid solidly beside me. I counted the holes in the mosquito net, easing into sleep, when he said it. "I want you to have a baby." It surfaced for the first time as a request a few days after the wedding. Now it had become a hard-nosed demand.

"How can we think of that now? We don't have our own house. You aren't working. We've little money."

"None of that matters," he said calmly, as though reading from a mental brief drawn up to counter my protests. "By the time the baby comes things will be in place."

"You've got to give me more time. I've been here three months. I haven't found my bearings yet."

"That's not important."

"But it is." My heart revved up like a motor out of control, terrified by the implications of his judgment. "You're saying what I feel means nothing."

"What I'm saying is that *here* children are wealth. People don't wait for the things you're talking about before having them." Never before had we talked about children. We just assumed—it then hit me, a swift, iron-fisted blow in the stomach—entirely different things. I, that we would wait. He, that waiting was unnecessary.

"Wealth?" I shouted. "What about the dirty, unschooled children filling this city's streets, performing a hundred different tasks just to survive. Whose wealth are they?"

"The wealth of families who depend on the money they bring home at night to buy bread and *gari*."

"But we aren't those people. We'll never be. And what about us?" I slid away from him as if in danger. "What about us?" The words screeched, hysterical. "I want to get a firm grasp on me, and especially you, before we have a child. Don't you understand? Can't you?"

A dark cloud of confusion passed over his face. He looked down at his hands and when he looked at me again his face was wrapped in barbed wire. "Children are required. Expected. You know that."

"Please, why can't we just wait? Six months, even." He stood up and dressed, silently stalking out of the room, leaving me in the middle of the bed, naked, trembling in the invisible emotional debris.

Already Sara had told me, in a lowered voice, stories of women who could not conceive and who bartered their souls in communion with juju men and sacrifices made to special gods. As she spoke I saw the contempt that scarred the faces of husbands, friends and family who wondered at such ill fortune. I imagined, too, the triumph of a fertile second wife, loved by family and adored even by the first wife because she bore children as ripe as fruit. And she told me tales, too, of women cursed because they bore only female children. For here the child becomes the woman, becomes the man. Bisi sacrificed her name and was called by all "*mami* Yemi" in honor of her daughter; her husband Jide proudly became "Baba Olu" for their son. I had watched Bisi fall to her knees, coaxing Olu out of an evil mood, stroking the prickly back of his anger with the words "*Oko mi, Oko mi*" ("my husband, my husband"), offering the boy a mock respect he would soon demand as a right. I recalled the anthropology books I read detailing the African belief that children symbolized ancestors returned to life. Endearing as that philosophy seemed on the pages of a book, at that moment it savagely encroached on my life.

In self-defense, each of us protecting his own ideal, our love-making became an undeclared war. I took a pill—minute saver of my soul—each day. Still, my legs were paralyzed, immobile, and

Femi had to force them apart to enter me. I cried silently, holding his weight, edited my passion so he could not touch me deeply enough to bring forth another life.

The policy was labeled "indigenisation." Foreign businesses and corporations were required by the Nigerian government to train Nigerians for management positions and to install them in jobs once held exclusively by expatriates. The ad in the *Daily Times* was for an architectural engineer for an American-owned construction firm five years in the country. At the initial interview Femi met the company's manager, John McElroy, who, he discovered, had attended his undergraduate alma mater. In an animated, warm conversation they talked about Long Island University, the United States, Nigeria's future, and the position being offered. McElroy was impressed, Femi said, and virtually assured him the job. A final interview before a panel of the now exclusively Nigerian board of directors was scheduled. Femi spent the days before that interview buoyed up by more hope than I'd seen in him since my arrival. He spent afternoons in the parlor, his sleeves rolled up, with old copies of *Fortune,* textbooks, blueprints, designs stacked around him. Poring over them, afternoon and night, he made up a list of questions he imagined he'd be asked and had me quiz him. The afternoon of the interview he left the house, looking snazzy in a three-piece suit. He had told family and friends the job was his, had wondered aloud at the salary and what type of car he would buy. The board consisted of four Nigerians and was headed by Mr. McElroy.

That evening he told me the interview went well, but the Nigerians' questions were shaped, it seemed, into traps to ensnare him. Occasionally they looked bored. And the tone of some of their questions were openly hostile. Only McElroy, he said, appeared objective and genuinely interested in his ideas. The next day a messenger brought a letter to him saying that the board had voted against him. In the note McElroy expressed surprise and dismay and added that he had cast the single vote in Femi's favor and had argued strenuously in his behalf.

"It was tribalism pure and simple," Femi said to Jide. We gathered in Jide's living room, Bisi with us, as Femi acknowledged this latest defeat. "I tell you, brother, that's all it could have been. There were three Igbos and one Hausa on the board. I never stood a chance. Mr. McElroy said they thought I couldn't handle the job." His voice quaked with indignation.

"You are probably right," Jide said, shaking his head sadly. "Will the old hatreds never be buried?" he asked aloud. "Give an Igbo man a job and within six months everyone in the office will be a cousin or a friend." Jide rose and stared at a picture on the wall of the former head of state. It was inscribed with Yoruba words that blessed him for keeping the nation united.

"Uncle," Bisi said softly, "you will be stronger for this."

Jide turned back to us, "You must put this behind you, Femi, and go on. You have a wife, your health. A job will come."

The next day Femi received requests for interviews from two other firms he had applied to. He bitterly tossed both letters into the trash. I retrieved them and begged him to at least consider one. "I don't need them anymore," he said, his eyes gleaming with a calm desperation. "From now on I'll make my own luck. My own future."

The next afternoon my three suitcases were stationed at the door to Femi's room. "Why are these here?" he asked, his body poised for a challenge.

"Because I'm moving in."

"I told you—"

"And now I'm telling you," I interrupted him. "I don't belong in Jide's house. He is not my husband."

"You're making me angry."

"I've made you angry before and you never took back your love." I planted my body firmly on the edge of the bed.

"I've asked you to give me time," he pleaded.

"I'm asking you to let me be your wife."

He floundered for an excuse. "There's no room. How will you get to school?"

"I won't negotiate for the right to love you, Femi. I've come too far, from my family, my friends."

He knelt on the floor before me. "But a friend and I have decided to start our own business. In a few more weeks—"

"I won't leave. And you won't throw me out."

Nettled by my determination, he looked at my bags and then at me. "Just for a few days," he insisted. "No longer than that. I don't care what you say."

Matthew appeared at the door. "Master, cook say you come eat now."

"Tell her I'm eating as well, Matthew," I declared. "Tell her from now on to prepare enough for two at each meal." I hoisted my bags onto the bed and removed my clothes, hanging them in the closet. I filled the drawers with underwear and lined the chest with bottles of makeup and cosmetics.

"I will let you stay," Femi concluded when I finished, his face shimmering with relief.

I grabbed his hand. "Come on, let's eat. I'm hungry."

Femi and an old friend from his hometown set up an architectural engineering firm. As manager of a British pools operation whose tiny offices dotted the city, Olu Akinyemi had made a small fortune. Femi had convinced him that with Lagos expanding and its population growing in quantum leaps, setting up a business to design/build housing and office space for those who needed it was not only logical but destined to succeed. The fact that the city had sprouted as many such firms as people who need their services did not daunt either of them. So his friend Olu Akinyemi invested seed money, while Femi provided the expertise. They opened shop on the second floor of a well-kept, neat building on a street whose residents were valiantly attempting to prevent it from becoming a slum.

Lagos teemed with ghettoes—Sabo, parts of Ebute Metta, Ajegunle, Moroko, where a dozen people sometimes shared one room, all living, sleeping and cooking in the same space. In these same slums a maze of television antennas perched atop roofs of corrugated tin. People who could barely speak English watched ten-year-old reruns of "Julia," "The Flip Wilson Show" and "Hawaii Five-O." Ironically—and with ominous frequency—whole sections of Lagos were without electricity for days, the government-run power company understaffed and ill-equipped. Landlords seemingly built apartment buildings overnight, neglecting to connect water pipes. So plastic containers of water, filled at roadside faucets, were packed inside the trunks of

Mercedes by lawyers or professors, or carried on the heads of house girls fending their way through the ever busy streets. Lagos was expanding like a seething monster, every inch of arable land claimed by a highway, a building or squatters. In the midst of this spirit-grinding chaos the middle-class couple searched for an apartment, the businessman for office space. Femi planned to give them just what they wanted.

I forged a dishonorable peace with him over the issue of a child. Easily, remarkably, I lied. "You are still having your period?" he asked, his eyes measuring the bloodstain smudging the sheet.

"Yes."

"But why? I told you to get rid of those pills."

"Femi, you don't get pregnant overnight."

"You're not still taking them, are you?"

"No." And as I uttered the word, I pictured the packet of pills lodged beneath a fifth form reader in my desk at school. On my lunch hour I pressed one against my tongue and swallowed it with a Coke. On Fridays I folded two of them, for Saturday and Sunday, inside a tissue and hid them in my purse. Surreptitiously I fought for my life.

"How long does it take," he asked shyly, "to make a baby?"

"Don't be so anxious," I teased him. "If you'd relax and stop worrying, maybe it would happen." I was amazed that I looked at his face unashamed, even as I deceived the trust staring back at me.

That night I had a dream. All the people I am went on a rampage. One of my selves calmly surveyed the rest of me—bickering and hungry, banging tin cups against the bar. The writer stood along the edge of the disturbance, taking notes, camouflaging her true identity. The teacher called the riot to order, clapped her hands, shouting "Ladies, please." The wife reached for her husband's hand while squirreling away morsels of her soul for the bad times. Suddenly *mother* burst through the barroom door. Thin ribbons of smoke slithered from the mouth of two pistols held in the air. "Everyone against the wall!" she screamed. All my other selves scrambled for cover but were hunted down beneath tables, dragged from behind locked bathroom doors, caught holding our breath in slender corners. Mother lassoed each one, dragged us across the splintered floor, tossed us into a heap in a corner. "Now yall *stay* there till I say you can move," she sneered, perching one booted and spurred foot on a nearby chair. Craning her neck, she scanned our faces for evidence of rebellion. Satisfied by our display of meekness, she sat down and struck a match on the sole of her boot. Between puffs on a cigar, she chuckled happily, "From now on this here town's gonna be mine."

Christmas. We made a pilgrimage to Femi's hometown, a five-hour drive from Lagos. Driving a car borrowed from the Chief, we passed through a host of towns—Ikorodu, which resembled an outpost; Ijebu-Ode, a Moslem stronghold; Ibadan, Ore, Ondo, Akure. As we drove along it, the highway on some parts of the journey was being laid down by a German contractor whose name was synonymous with new roads in the country. We drove over months-old stretches of roads he had built, already buckling and warping, crater-filled from the pressure of cars and trucks. Tiny hamlets nestled behind the trees and thick foliage yards from the road. From there children made forays onto the side of the highway, where they hawked bottles of Ogogoro, a strong native liquor that some say is so hearty only men can drink it.

Femi was born in a sun-baked town of steep hills sloping into stiff red-clay peaks and valleys. Ado-Ekiti was patient. Quiet. Villagelike in the endurance of human bond and concern. The town, once proud, now stood depleted of most of its youth, lost to Nigeria's cities. His mother still lived in the two-room house in which she was born. The same house in which she lived as the wife of Femi's father. I was told that as his wife she sometimes heard her husband's voice, when angry, roll thunderlike across the hill blocking the view of his house from hers. His voice arrived, an unwelcome visitor rapping sharply against her door. Out of the close space were carved two rooms, a clay-floor hallway and a wizened back courtyard that was kitchen, laundry and shower. Nubile black-coated goats pranced through the hallway, littering it with the tiny pods of their waste.

My palms sweated against the bright paper of the gift I brought her while Femi conversed in Yoruba with one of his half sisters. He paced the floor nervously, his face creased with anxiety. Every few minutes he cast a worried look toward the corner where I sat squirming and nervous. Suddenly a hoarse, abandoned laugh burst from the rear of the house. Footsteps bounded toward the front. Seconds later she stood before me, a tall, dark woman, her body all angles and points, her head swathed in a simple *galae,* a wooden chewing stick perched between her teeth. A broad smile conquered her face and she blessed me with a look of curious, undisguised appreciation. The room exploded with Yoruba as she asked Femi all about me. Turning back to me, she smiled again, and in a singsong rhythm said "*Oyingbo, oyingbo*" ("Foreigner, foreigner"). Yet it did not sound like hard mocking, as when thrown like a stone by children in the market, but rather like a secret she had discovered and now gladly divulged to the world. I bowed on one knee before her. Lowering my head, I caught a glimpse of Femi's face, proud and pleased as he watched me. Rising from the floor, I clasped her hand. My palm felt the same strength and hope present in the touch of my mother's fingers—shorter, wider, less gnarled by work and time than those gripping mine at that moment. She took the gift I offered. Removing the watch from the box, she slid it onto her narrow wrist. Extending her hand stiffly, she said, "Thank you." The only English phrase she knew.

From Bisi I learned that, though illiterate, Femi's mother was a woman of grace and intelligence. Perhaps *because* she spent her years as wife in a polygamous marriage, she urged her three sons never to take more than one wife. With the other wives and children she worked her husband's farm, and on her own she gained financial independence as a trader of cloth and foodstuffs. Instrumental in sending both Femi and Jide—adored, spoiled, respected because of their manhood—to universities abroad, she sat in waiting for their success. Girlish, supremely proud, behind her smile she nurtured a self-possession bequeathed in ample supply to her offspring.

At dinner Femi's face beamed love toward his mother and approval at me. He told her of the business he and Olu had started and she listened carefully, suggesting, probing, encouraging. They were intimate and honest as lifelong friends. Fluttering around us, she urged me to eat, laughing when I coughed because of the hot pepper in the stew. Her gentle, deep laughter danced beneath the dim, kerosene-lit darkness. It was the laugh of all the black women I had ever known.

There was only one bed in the house, so after dinner Femi said, "You will sleep here tonight. I will sleep in my father's house."

I quaked at the thought of being alone with her. Yet after the house girl washed the dishes and lit the kerosene lamps for the night, Femi's mother sat down beside me and asked in Yoruba about my family. She spoke Yoruba heavily tinged with the Ekiti dialect of the town. I answered her in the Yoruba I had gleaned from a textbook written by a British linguist, and which had in the past three months been molded by the sound of Lagos Yoruba, a hodgepodge of various vernaculars. "*Baba mi ati mama mi won ti ku,*" I said, telling her my parents were dead.

"*Pele, pele,*" she comforted me, touching my shoulder.

I told her how Femi and I met in America. About my mother and her houses, and about my father and the tales he told me of Africa. She liked the stories of my mother best and asked if my father had other wives. I laughed, remembering the other women who claimed his loyalty as fiercely as my mother, but finally smiled grimly and said, "No, she was the only one." For an hour we sat, two women before a flickering lamp in a room hushed by darkness, exchanging bits of lives neither could fully comprehend but merely struggle to respect.

Morning broke open clean and crisp. In the 5 A.M. darkness Femi's mother rose from the small cot we shared and fell on her knees in prayer. Clutching a small Bible, her voice was fervent, her body moving like a wave gripped by righteousness, as she prayed in the room's early-morning gloom. I feigned sleep, my back turned to her, and wondered at this once polygamous woman praying to Jesus Christ.

The house of Femi's father was massive and many-roomed. Three stories high with twisting, narrow stairways and cavernous halls, it sprawled atop one of the town's steepest hills. During a tour of the house four of the old man's widows, withered, gray and toothless, fluttered around me like small birds feasting on an unexpected meal. The source of his father's affluence was a twenty-five-acre farm worked chiefly by his wives and children. In honor of his leadership and contributions to the community he was made a chief. In a photograph on the wall of the man's bedroom he was dressed in elegant ceremonial robes, speaking by microphone to an unseen crowd. Without doubt Femi was his father's child, for the same distance and pride shone brilliantly in the man's eyes. I said aloud, *"O lewa pupa"* ("He is very handsome"), and the eyes of the man's widows collectively flashed to his face in reverence. I met one of the father's brothers, who, as caretaker of the house, said a prayer each morning for the dead man's spirit. Throughout the house elaborately carved head-stones marked the graves of members of the Ajayi family.

The lives of the deceased and the living were intertwined in a manner mundane and divine, for the graves were often situated beside a stove or work area.

Late afternoon. Femi took me to the house of his mother's brother, a retired civil servant living on a small pension. "Come, sit beside me," he gently commanded, patting the space next to him on the wooden bench. The scent of strong native liquor laced his breath. Formidable in size and presence, he sat dressed in faded, slightly tattered robes. "Welcome to my country," he said, touching my cheek with a large hand. "You are West Indian," he concluded, eyeing me quizzically for a moment.

"No, uncle, she is from America," Femi explained.

The man's mouth opened slowly in surprise, forming a perfect circle. "But she looks like us." He rubbed my skin as if to test the hue, then tightened his grip on my hand for confirmation. "Ahhhh . . . so we Africans are in America as well?" The question came in a whisper. "You have brought one of our own back from the land of the whites, Femi. And you will stay," he said to me firmly. "You belong here. To us."

I lay my hand over his, basking in the intent of his words and touch. Stating what I was certain was a vow, I answered, "Yes, uncle, I will stay."

To celebrate Christmas family members converged on Ado-Ekiti from Ife and Ibadan, stopping first at the house of Femi's mother to pay respects. Most often she held court in the backyard, where the real living was done. In the afternoon I watched her kill a goat for the evening feast. While two women held the goat, tethered front and hind legs, she slit the throat, then shaved the hair with a razor and singed the flesh with a torch to destroy germs. An hour later the goat turned on a spit over a fire in the center of the courtyard. Busy with important but unhonored tasks, the other women peeled yams and ground tomatoes and peppers on a stone. In the evenings, as relatives filled the house, my mother-in-law happily thrust me into their midst.

The next day Ado-Ekiti witnessed a marriage ceremony, and the atmosphere was festive for this joining of families. The family of the groom came to the bride's tiny wood-splintered house to fetch her. Repeatedly the groom's father knocked on the wooden door for entry, while his wife called the name of the bride and asked if anyone was at home. But in reply the bride's family pretended not to know them, as custom required, refusing to give up their daughter easily. The bride's sister peeked through the front door, giggling as she interrogated the groom's relatives. Finally the bride's family relented and the bride came out, followed by younger sisters, relatives and her father's three wives. The bride was the same "sewing mistress" I had seen the day before sitting in a small shop before an old-fashioned sewing machine. Her blouse and wrapper were emerald green and white, and gold bracelets shimmered like snakes along both arms. Gold earrings dangled nearly to her shoulders. Poised and smiling, she undulated down the path outside her door, the groom's family beaming happily at her. The bride's four sisters trailed behind the bride, carrying her clothing and personal effects in baskets perched on their heads. Other relatives followed the sisters, the hems of the men's flowing robes making trails in the dusty road. The wives of the bride's father came last, each rotund, strutting, as regal as the bride herself. This caravan marched gaily through the town, progressing over its steep hills, before a crowd of well-wishers gathered along the route. The bride's sisters and her father's wives sang as they marched in the procession, their voices a happy chorus wishing the bride farewell. From the back of the line the senior wife asked, *"Kilense li e fi po b'awonyi o'?"* ("What are you doing that you are so many?") The others, forming a chorus, responded:

Chorus: We are taking a new wife. Listen to the sound of the beads, great sound of beads. We are taking a new wife.

Senior wife: Congratulations to the bride and bridegroom.

Chorus: Congratulations to the bride and bridegroom.

Senior wife: May the bride not be childless.

Chorus: May the bride not be childless.

Senior wife: Thanks to the bridegroom for today's ceremony.

Chorus: Thanks to the bridegroom for today's ceremony.

Senior wife: Sympathize with the other unlucky man.

Chorus: Sympathize with the other unlucky man.

Once at the groom's house, the bride sat on a stool that awaited her, stationed before the front door. One of her sisters knelt before her to wash her feet with water brought in a bowl by the groom's sister. Symbolically any transgressions from the past were washed away before she stepped into the home of her new family. Her feet clean, the bride stood and entered the house where her husband waited.

Femi loaded the trunk of the car with a dozen large tubular yams, a small mountain of bananas, mangoes, a supply of pineapples and bushmeat wrapped in newspaper. I stood watching him as his mother called to me from the doorway, "Ayo," the Yoruba name she gave me. It meant joy, and she had named me after herself. I followed her purposeful stride into the bedroom. Kneeling before her, I thanked her for welcoming me and asked when she would come to Lagos. She did not know. Proudly she refused the gift of money I offered her at Femi's instruction, merely taking it and then pressing the bills firmly back into my palm. Her interests lay elsewhere. Piercing me with a gaze I could not escape, she asked when we would have a child.

"Soon," I whispered hurriedly, looking away from her. Then I kissed her cheek and ran from the room, hurrying outside to join Femi in the car. Settling against the front seat, I wondered at the doggedness with which the request haunted me, steadily becoming a nightmare from which I feared I would never wake.

15

The afternoon sky was indecisive. All morning it had trembled between clouds and sunlight. The clouds did not threaten rain, for the rainy season was months away. Rather, they seemed to conceal what the sudden appearance of the sun attempted to unveil.

Walking out of the school's compound at noon, one of the girls in my fourth form class ran toward me hysterically, shouting, "They're killing themselves! They're killing themselves!" tears streaming down her cheeks.

"What's happened?" I asked her. But she broke out of my grasp and bolted toward the school, still shouting her warning. More puzzled than frightened, I walked toward Awolowo Road, which was lined with an unusually heavy flow of traffic. The cars stretched as far as I could see and the people inside them appeared edgy and expectant, craning their necks out of car windows, looking in all directions. Horns honked, sounding jittery and upset. At a BP gasoline station next to the store where I bought my lunch every day, a dark green army vehicle lay immobilized like a wounded animal. Its tires were flat, the front and side windows shattered by a gestalt image of bullet holes. A deserted jeep squatted ominously a few feet away. It was then that I noticed that the normally crowded sidewalks were virtually empty, as was the parking lot outside Barclays Bank.

Clutching my handbag, I ran back to the school. On entering the compound, I met the entire population, students and staff, standing on the grounds. The headmaster ran up to me, panting with excitement. "Mrs. Ajayi, where have you been? Don't you know there's been a coup attempt?"

"But how? Where?" I stammered.

Pointing in an eastward direction, he said, "Surely you know that the army barracks is within walking distance of us. They say it started there." Before my feelings of apprehension could gel, the school was dismissed for the rest of the day.

I immediately ran to Sara's office a block away. "What does it all mean?" I asked.

"That's what we don't know yet," she said, seating me in a chair beside her desk.

"How can you remain so calm?" I asked impatiently, feeling like a firecracker about to explode. I looked around the office, the Nigerians manning rows of desks, talking quietly among themselves but continuing to work. The European managers fidgeted behind mammoth desks in their executive offices, leaving their doors partially open.

"Remember, I've lived through one coup attempt and the rest of these people have seen even more." A radio sat atop a desk in the middle of the office. Suddenly the music stopped as the voice of the ringleader of the conspiracy crackled in the air. Martial music played in the background as he announced, with the voice of a man half-clown, half-maniac, that the government had been seized and the head of state killed. The Nigerians circled uneasily around the radio. Some laughed in the wake of his pronouncement, most were indifferent. They had heard all this before and seemed more resigned and amused than anxious. The speech rambled on, long and obscene, the voice razor-sharp one moment, whimpering the next, pumping me full of fear. A sob rumbled across my throat and I burst into tears. Sara led me back into her office, offering me a wad of tissues.

Minutes later the manager told everyone they could go home. Sara and I dashed for her car. Awolowo Road was still jammed. The city was simultaneously tense and unperturbed, and intermittently we saw soldiers, individually or in groups, on the streets. That evening Femi and I sat around the radio in the Chief's living room. All day long friends had come in with a new rumor, a new speculation. Periodically the plotters announced they had control of the entire country; an hour later the claim would be denied by broadcasts from the North and East by government soldiers. By dusk it was clear that though the head of state and several top-ranking officers had indeed been killed, the coup attempt had failed. At nine o'clock the former chief of staff made a speech on television revealing details of the plot and announcing that he had been chosen to take over leadership of the country.

In a mere seven months Muritala Mohammed had gained a respect from his countrymen that crossed tribal boundaries. Stern and tough, he had by all his actions, from the mass firing of corrupt civil servants to the creation of several new states to ease ethnic tensions, issued a charge to Nigeria to finally become the country it smugly thought it already was. His death in February 1976 provoked an outpouring of emotion and calls for unity that heartened everyone concerned over the country's future.

For three days after his death Lagos' skys were dark. Rain fell heavy and unremitting. Still, students filled the streets with demonstrations; some were peaceful, mourning the death of Mohammed, while others were bitter, angrily ransacking the British embassy, burning the flag and charging the British government with a hand in the plot.

Within weeks thirty-six plotters had been arrested, tried and convicted. While they were from all ranks in the Army and represented a number of different tribes, evidence surfaced that seemed to implicate the former head of state, General Gowon, in what appeared to be an attempt by him to regain power. The

Nigerian Government tried without success to extradite him from exile in Britain. The British Government's refusal to send Gowon back for trial strained relations between the two countries almost to the breaking point.

The executions of one group of conspirators was televised one evening, sandwiched between the news and a locally produced soap opera. This perverse use of imported technology amazed my sensibilities. The executions took place at Bar Beach on the mainland, where, since early morning, a crowd had been gathering to witness the carrying out of justice. Femi and I watched the television coverage; he was brooding and silent, in mourning for the death of something vital in his country that he could no longer find. I sat speechless and disbelieving. A camera panned the crowd, a surprising mix of classes and conditions. They mimicked, clowned for the camera. Some waved. Others hid their faces. All waited for the moment of national catharsis that would arrive with the sound of bullets exploding in the men's hearts. The men were tied to thick staffs stuck in the sand. Gratefully the camera scanned them from a distance. A priest blessed each one in turn. Then the voice of an off-camera commander called the soldiers to attention and ordered them to aim and fire. The men crumpled like rag dolls and the crowd roared its approval. I felt no catharsis, however, only embarrassment and sorrow as I slumped in the chair—as if I, too, had been shot—watching Femi turn the television off and leave the room in disgust.

Our apartment was in a part of Lagos in which houses popped up overnight. It was lodged on a back street, accessible from the main road by a maze of twists and turns. After depositing six months' rent in advance—all the money I had saved from teaching—we moved in. With the remaining money brought from the States I bought furniture. The landlord was petulant, spoke in rapid bursts and had the look of a gangster. He and his family inhabited the entire top floor of the six-unit building. His wife, a wealthy "cash madam," owned a store in Lagos that sold cloth. Relatives from her town made up the household staff; they milled about in the back and front of the house all day and even at night, washing clothes, preparing food, bathing children, living as in the village. Our next-door neighbors were a couple recently returned from Britain. Amazingly, we had water. There were three bedrooms and I claimed one room as a study. I lined its walls with the books shipped from the States, which were a map of my life. Femi rarely entered my study; he seemed threatened by the room with my name written all over its space. Encouraged by Sidney Offit, my fiction professor at N.Y.U., I had started a novel inspired by all the people and experiences I had known. Distilling, selecting from remembrance and dream, I conjured up characters that I prayed were real enough to meet on a street corner, to care for and love. I began the adventure, sure that I was mistress of my characters' souls, but soon they usurped much of my power, began dictating their fate, and soon spoke in a language I deciphered only because they inspired it. Some mornings I rose at 4 A.M., possessively claiming the new day, for at that time of the morning the world belonged to me. During my entire stay in Nigeria I struggled to give life to the people on those pages. They were never to claim an existence between hard covers, but they performed the tasks of all good friends—they kept me sane. They made me whole.

Inside our house I built the life I had been waiting for. I stopped taking the pill, ready, finally, to give myself up to the implications of our life together. My marriage became an emotional fortress. In the evening, when Femi came home and I heard the engine of his car, my heart, just like Bisi's, stood at attention. After dinner we watched television, and by ten o'clock we were in bed. It was a small life, the only life I wanted then. The sheer monotony of it was comforting, narcotic. And it was the knowing, the certainty that pleased me, for I was hibernating and shunned adventure. I was happy, knowing that, as Baba Tunji, who christened Taiwo and Kehinde, had said of Nike and Tope, "This is the way a marriage should be." As silent and as sure as the ticking of a clock.

"*Ekuaaro*, madam." Yetunde bent down on one knee and sprang back to a standing position. She quickly swallowed the rest of her *gari* and water, slurping it loudly from a bowl. She was sent by Femi's mother to be our house girl.

"*Pele*, Yetunde," I answered. At sixteen she was large-breasted yet still gangly, but when we walked from the market—she with a basket on her head, I behind her—the sensual swaying of her hips hinted at the woman she would soon be.

I pulled my own loincloth tighter around my chest, for at seven o'clock the morning still wore a chill. Since six her movements had resounded throughout the apartment. Waking, she folded up the straw mat on which she slept and placed it in the closet. Then she swept the entire house, dusting furniture, setting the table. Opening the refrigerator, I took out eggs, bread and milk. I spoke to her in Yoruba and English. Literal communication was no problem. But I remained awkward in this role of authority, either giving her too much work to do or not enough. Femi assured me I would feel easier as a "madam" in time. I was not so sure.

The apartment sat in darkness. For a week our neighborhood had been without electricity. Yetunde had lit kerosene lamps, placing them around the apartment. The heat, oppressive and moist, made it difficult even to breathe. Femi's key rattled in the door.

"Still no light?" he asked, his face showing astonishment.

"I went to the power company today," I told him. "They said a cable was damaged by one of the companies rebuilding Ikorodu Road."

"This is madness," he fumed, tossing his briefcase onto the sofa. Furious, he stripped off his shirt. "This is a country where nothing works. You can have a heart attack from the traffic. And you come home to eat dinner in the dark. Tell me, where's the progress? It wasn't this bad before I left."

Yetunde padded into the living room and knelt in greeting to him. "*Ekuale*, sir."

"*Pele*. I won't eat now. It's too hot," he said, and turned to go back out to the front porch. "Come join me," he said.

The night had no pulse, and because of the absence of power the darkness sank, murky and unrelieved, before our eyes. Barechested, he leaned over the banister. "When I was a child we would sit around the kerosene lamp on nights like this and tell stories and tales," he said, his voice wistful with sudden remembering. "We would be tired from a long day of working my father's farm, from six in the morning to six at night. All his wives and children. We used broken, rusted hoes to plant the yams, for my father rarely bought new tools, preferring to use what we had until it wore out. After dinner the children would play outside before being called to bed. My grandmother or some other elder would call us together and ask if we wanted to hear a story. We always did."

"What kind of stories were they?" I asked, moving closer to him, relishing these secrets he was divulging.

"Tales of tribal wars, myths, deeds of bravery. The history of my family."

"On summer nights like this one I played tag and hide-and-seek outside our house, and with my friends I caught fireflies in glass jars," I said. "My father told me stories, too, on nights like this. We'd sit on the front stoop and he'd tell me about Paul Robeson or George Washington Carver. He'd explain the words I'd heard on the news—communism, integration. He'd explain how they sent rockets into space. For a long time I thought he knew everything."

Femi rested his hand on my shoulder, gently kneading, caressing. Whispering so softly I could barely hear him, he said, "I am proud of you. You have done well, by my family and by me. We all thank you."

I heard through a friend of Sara's that the Department of Mass Communication at the University of Lagos had several lecturer positions for which they were seeking applicants. I had an interview with the chairman of the department, who immediately offered me a job. But the ensuing red tape stalled the hiring process for nearly five months. In the middle of the spring term I was finally officially hired. I resigned my position at the Lagos Comprehensive Girls' School and became, with a great deal of fanfare, surprise, and congratulations from Femi's family, a university professor.

The head of the department, Dr. Alfred Opubor, had recently returned from the States, where for eight years he headed an African studies program at a midwestern university. Possessed of an abundance of wit, charm, and intelligence, he had the distinction of being a male feminist. He juggled several occupational hats—hosting a weekly interview program on the radio, during which he talked to artists, scholars and scientists; running the department; teaching; delivering speeches on such topics as the role of women in developing countries; and serving as chairman of the board of his state's newspaper. He thrived on this conglomeration of interests, and because of his energy and the range of his talents I became an immediate fan. I was the only female professor in the department. My colleagues had all studied in American schools and were evenly split between communicologists, who propounded and researched mass communication theory, and those with a more professional orientation.

The student body of the university was overwhelmingly male, with perhaps 10 to 15 percent of the population being women. And there were only a handful of women lecturers. Very quickly I learned to adopt a stern, officious manner in the classroom, for I was initially taken less seriously than my male colleagues. Yet simultaneously I began to feel a bond with my students. They had run a gauntlet of tests to gain entry to a university that, like the few others in the country, had room for no more than a quarter of its applicants. They were bright, but even more, they were self-possessed. They were an elite and they knew it. They graduated to become government officials, editors of newspapers, molders of their own futures. They lived inside skins as dark as my own, but their skins simply did not, could not, imagine defeat. In my heart I applauded them, in my lectures I egged them on to success, with the pen that graded their papers I told them never to rest until they had done their best. I taught journalism and English, and to the two or three female students in each class I became a role model. Surreptitiously they courted my friendship and in my office they worried over grades and shared with me the blueprints they had drawn of their lives. Some were studious and scholarly, while others were homespun and meek. And then there were those labeled "acada girls," hothouse flowers dotting the campus landscape. They wore makeup and looked sleek in stylish clothes bought on holidays in London. Their youth and education made them prized possessions. So they were pursued by the "big men" in business, the civil service, and the Army, who collected them as mistresses and girl friends. At night and on weekends a caravan of Volvos and Mercedes and some army vehicles stretched outside the girls' dormitories. Inside the "acada girls" were courted, enticed and bought.

After my last class, Ikpoi Ogboi passed me in the hall. "Come, Mrs. Ajayi, join me for a beer in the staff club."

"Alright, just let me drop off my books," I told him, grateful for the invitation. Ogboi was forthright and entertaining.

Having returned two months earlier from Syracuse University, where he successfully defended his doctoral thesis, he swaggered with just enough pompousness to make him interesting. Now he glowed in the wake of his promotion to senior lecturer. Afternoons he charged into the office I shared with Mr. Oyewale and regaled us with blasphemous anecdotes about the new regime or, after a night spent without electricity, memories of the efficiency of America. While some were intrigued or offended by my Americanness, Ogboi was openly attracted to it, peppering his speech with American slang. Winking in confidence at me, he would tell a joke that was typically American in flavor. An Igbo living among Yorubas, for sheer survival he became proficient in a number of ethnic languages, expertly absorbing the sound and sometimes the values of his surroundings like a protective coloring. Ambitious and aggressive, he was in the process of muting all that with savvy.

"You know, I always found you sisters in America a puzzle," he said, taking purposely slow steps as we walked toward the staff club.

"How do you mean?" I looked at him sharply, tensing at the edge imprinted on the sound of "sisters."

"Well, it was funny—" he began.

I thought of his wife, Ann, auburn hair and blue eyes. We met at a birthday party for one of the black American girls. She was friendly, easy to talk to. But I did not know whether timidity or overconfidence imbued her with the aura of a princess.

"You were so conscious of color," Ikpoi continued, "of how

dark or how light one was." I looked at his face—ebony-hued and broad-featured, a face I found appealing because of its unequivocal blackness.

"I went to a school in the South, before you discovered black was beautiful, and I was amazed at the obsession with color. It was subtle. It was obvious. But you could never escape it."

"Ikpoi, I don't know what to say. I'm not responsible for anyone else. I'll only apologize, if need be, for what I do."

"And then, when I went to grad school at Syracuse, if I went out to a party with a white girl, the sisters spread it all over the campus and made me an outcast."

"Did you marry your wife because no black woman would have you?" I asked, proud of my straightforwardness.

"I married her because I love her." We walked in silence for a few moments, our appetites for revelation perked. "In the States, would you have shunned me because of Ann?" he asked.

"I'd have found it unsettling. Hard to accept. I'd have felt betrayed. You are black, after all, and belong to me."

He stopped in mid stride, seemingly offended by my claim. Shaking his head, he laughed. "That's preposterous."

"No, Ikpoi, it's the truth."

16

The rainy season invaded the city and occupied it like a marauding army. At night rain hammered against the roof a thousand wet blows. The sound of nature's cadence lulled me to sleep. The scent of tropical rain lingered long after it had stopped. It cracked open the land, releasing the aroma of red clay—muddy, slick and gleaming; filled the air with the scent of pineapples—moist, perched on wooden stalls. All day a pallor dripped from the sky and swathed the city. Rain drenched, fed the crops and burrowed into the spirit. It was fickle, arriving in sudden, intense bursts, a downpour lasting minutes. It was a fine mist, bothersome yet invisible, plunging the city's soul into neurosis. And Lagos became a river, its different sections tributaries vainly forded by cars, pedestrians, motorcycles, mammy wagons, tankers. Cars were deserted, stuck in the streams and ponds that flooded the roads. Vehicles dotted the face of the city. The "go-slow" was twisted into bulging knots at Yaba, Apapa, and Maryland; it crept, snarling and befuddled, all day and into the night.

Anita Okunwunmi's house was starched and pressed. We sat on a plush velour sofa in her living room, which was opulent and overdressed. Along two walls stretched a stereo, tape deck, color television and videocassette recorder. A silver tray on the bar held a collection of liquors, wines and fine cut glasses. The room, like the entire apartment, which occupied the top floor of the building, smelled plastic, untouched. As my eyes scanned the room, I wondered what kind of life unfolded on such a stage. On the way over, Sara had told me that Anita's husband traveled often to Europe and America on business, that he had been awarded government contracts to import rice and meat.

"Aren't those contracts hard to get?" I asked.

"Money talks as loud here as anywhere else," she said simply. As she parked outside the house, in front of Anita's Audi, she observed, "I'll confess, I envy everything they own. But I feel sorry for the life they live."

"What do you mean?" I asked, but she shushed me quickly, pointing to Anita waving from the balcony.

I sat watching Anita unwrap the birthday gift Sara had brought her. Her manicured, perfectly lacquered nails untied the ribbon neatly and unstuck the Scotch tape. She was as well dressed as the apartment, and I sensed that the clothes, the furniture—everything—attempted, with only partial success, to hide some wound that opened without warning, gushing blood and tears.

The box sat unopened in her lap. She looked up at Sara. "Let me guess, an easel."

"Not quite," Sara laughed.

Opening the box, Anita lifted a handful of paintbrushes, all with thick, tufted edges, and a set of sketching pencils. "Oh, Sara, how'd you know I'd run out of them?"

Looking at the wall, Sara said, "That picture of Banji has been up there alone too long." Over the television hung a painting of Anita's husband done in oils. "I'll come and sit for my portrait anytime," she added.

Anita ran the brushes across the palm of her hand, and lovingly squeezed the hairs between her fingers. "Now, if I can just get in the mood to paint again." And then she said, "Let me get you something to drink. Ronke," she called.

"Ma?" a slouching, irritable voice answered from the kitchen. "Come here."

We heard the slamming of pots and pans and then the slow shuffle of bare feet against the cement floor coming toward us. "Ma?" the girl asked, hovering at the entrance to the living room, lips pursed. She did not look at Anita. She did not, in fact, look at any of us but fixed her stare on a blank space on the wall, her face bunched in discontent.

"Bring three Cokes and put ice in the glasses, on a tray," Anita said.

The girl turned and Sara said authoritatively, "*Pele* Ronke."

Shamefaced, Ronke turned and hung her head, bowing on one knee to Sara. "*Ekabo, Mama Sade,*" she said, and then blushed and scurried to the kitchen.

"You handle your house girls so well, Sara," Anita moaned. "I don't know what I do wrong. I still can't get used to being called madam."

Ronke brought the tray of drinks, setting them carefully on the table. We settled back in our chairs and I looked at Anita's face. We had met at parties, run into each other in stores. But for the first time I saw the anguish hidden among the collage of emotions stamped on her face. It was as though she had been frightened very badly and had retreated into mute acceptance. Her smile was a nervous twitch she could not seem to control. The large moon-shaped eyes reflected pain. She sat before us, her legs folded beneath her, her hands absently picking at her dress. We shifted in the silence. She no longer seemed to realize we were there, and I felt her slipping out of our grasp.

"So, how is everything? Work?" Sara asked, struggling to bring her back to us.

"Alright," she shrugged. "I'm thinking of quitting."

"Why?"

"I don't know," she shrugged again. "I haven't really decided yet."

"You know Judy went back home last week. She's going to grad school to get her doctorate," Sara told her.

"And Michael let her go?" Anita whispered in surprise.

"Well, she took the kids, and she wants to finish up in two years if she can."

"Is she coming back?"

"She said she would."

"When I go home every year, you know, I always say I won't come back," Anita brooded, almost to herself, "and I always do. Banji meets me at the airport and there's always a trace of surprise on his face when he sees me coming through customs. He's no more surprised than me."

Smoothing over the bumps this soliloquy raised, Sara bustled in her chair. "We're on our way to visit Janet. She had her baby yesterday."

"Oh, what hospital?"

"A clinic in Ebute-Metta."

Anita stood up slowly. "Tell her I'll come visit her. But, then again, maybe you shouldn't. Just give her my love."

In the car Sara told me that Anita's husband had a second wife.

"You're kidding," I gasped. She shook her head adamantly. "But why?"

"She can't have children. The family put pressure on him to find someone who could. The other wife has given him two boys."

"And she stays?" I sputtered angrily. "How can she still love him?"

"I'm not sure she does. She's miserable, but she needs him."

"When did all this happen?"

"Just a few years ago. The husband held out against the family as long as he could; then, after they'd been here three years and still hadn't had a child, he gave in. They went to several doctors in the States. She had a botched abortion when she was sixteen. Her tubes are badly scarred."

"A second wife," I whispered, amazed. The second wife was the nightmare that raged against the locked door of all our hearts. Wondering at the empathy I felt for Anita, whom I hardly knew, I remembered that we American wives were a clan in exile. "And what about her husband? What does he feel? What can he?"

"He is a happy man now." Sara laughed hard and bitterly, starting the engine. "He has an American wife and two sons. What more could he want?"

Femi's brother Kunle spent the year after his graduation from secondary school with his brother Jide in Lagos. For several months he lived with Jide, then he traveled back to Ado-Ekiti. He returned to Lagos to continue preparing for the college entrance exams and to search for a job. A cousin returned home from study in England and stayed with Jide until he was settled, so Kunle moved in with us. His distaste for me endowed him with a power that he used with joyful capriciousness. He called me "madam," saying it with the distance of a servant to a master. If I were Yoruba, he would have called me by the name of my children, and if there were no children, he would have called me sister. But I was called "madam" and the word became a wedge between us. When I heard it, as when he announced that he was going out or asked, "Where is my brother?" I thought of English women reclining on verandas, sipping tea, while the Matthews and Yetundes of the world scurried around them.

At Femi's insistence I tutored Kunle in English, the test he most feared failing. After each session he complained that my accent made it impossible for him to understand me. He was an obstacle course I would not maneuver my way through. His impatience reminded me that though I spoke his language and ate his food, I still lived inside myself in a room neither he nor Femi could enter, one which I knew not how to open.

Femi reminded me that Kunle felt awkward in my presence. "He has not known any foreigners before and does not quite know how to act."

"I heard him tell Yetunde the other day that he wished you had married that Yoruba girl instead of me," I responded.

"Yes," Femi nodded, "because then he would know how to treat you and what was expected of him. With you he is not sure."

The cheese had sat on a plate in the refrigerator for three days. I had planned to cook macaroni and cheese and surprise Femi, who enjoyed a change from our steady diet of stew and starchy native dishes as much as I did. Walking into the kitchen, I saw Kunle at the table, cutting something with a knife. "Kunle, what are you doing?" When he turned, I saw the cheese, a knife splitting it in half. "Kunle, that cheese belongs to me. I want to use it for dinner tonight."

Pulling his tall frame ramrod straight, he stood before me, defiant, his large hand holding the fat wedge of cheese. "This is my brother's house and I can eat anything in it."

"That's *my* cheese and nobody can have it, except your brother, without asking me first."

He dropped the cheese back onto the plate as though it stung his hand. "You're in Africa now," he warned me, seething with anger. "And you have to do things the way we do them here. What belongs to my brother belongs to me."

"Well, that cheese doesn't belong to Femi and I don't want you to touch it." He barged out of the house, the glass door nearly shattering. I looked at the cheese, his fingerprints embedded all over it, the crumbs of it scattered around the plate, and I tossed it in the garbage.

That night Femi confronted me. "Kunle told me what happened."

"He doesn't like me."

"He's a small boy. A child. I expect more of you."

"But why couldn't he have asked for it first? I wouldn't have said no."

"He should not have to ask. By our custom, he doesn't have to. No friend or relative must ask for anything first, especially my brother."

"I am your wife," I reminded him.

"Anyway," he shrugged, "I have told him to respect your wishes."

"So, I will never be *iyawo* (wife)."

"No. Bisi is *iyawo* to Jide and to us all. You are my wife alone."

When Femi's friends visited us, they settled heartily into the house, shouting "*Ekuale iyawo.*" I responded with a smile and a pleasant, mocking, "*Ekabo* (sir)," bowing slightly. Instantly they consigned me to the kitchen, asking in playful surprise, "Where is the pounded yam?" *Iyawo*—wife to husband and spiritual wife to his family. The name fit me like a noose, and as I removed it from my neck I reached for the identity it took me so long to mold at home.

Suddenly I needed to be reassured. "Do you love me?" I asked. "Say it. Tell me," I demanded, feeling parched, aching with an incredible chasmlike need.

"You would not be here if I didn't."

"Why is it so hard to say?"

"What has this to do with my brother? You aren't a child," he said defensively.

"No. I'm a woman who needs at this moment, more than anything else, to hear you say you care."

"Alright, I love you," he conceded, quickly turning his attention back to the television screen. The words landed like an egg breaking against the floor, and they sounded like death. I wanted to pick them up and throw them at him, stuff them down his throat until he gagged. Instead, I went to the bedroom, undressed, burrowing beneath the sheets. When he came to bed, I resented the possessiveness of his touch and pretended I was asleep.

But Kunle's discontent increased and he began to be rude and short with Femi. When Femi told him to wash the car, he performed the task sluggishly, grumbling as he did it. He came in late and began to lie. Finally, one morning the explosion came. Femi wanted to get into the bathroom and Kunle refused to hurry and finish. In a rage, Femi pushed the door in, breaking the lock, his elbow gashed by a splintered seam in the door. Kunle stood before the sink, a towel around the lower part of his body. "I said come out!" Femi shouted, grabbing him by the neck like a puppy and pulling him into the hallway. He threw him against the wall and began slapping him. "I told you to come out. I told you to come out."

As tall as Femi but slender, Kunle shielded his face with his arms and hands, shouting, "Stop, brother. Help."

The boy's cries only fueled Femi's rage. He used his hands, knees and elbows against the boy, pounding him with an explosion of frustration, filling the hallway with the sound of thuds and screams. Yetunde stood beside me and fell on her knees to Femi, begging him in Pidgin English, "*Ejo, oga,* make u stop, make u stop, you go kill am, you go kill am." She was wringing her hands, slapping her thighs and holding her stomach as though feeling each blow. "Make u stop *oga!*" she screamed.

The fierceness of the attack stunned and immobilized me. I felt vindicated by it, some part of my own honor defended by this righteous anger. But I was afraid of it as well, and my fear snipped out my tongue and froze me to the kitchen doorway, my hand holding a spoon dripping stew onto the floor. I had never seen this Femi, overwhelming and monstrous, in full dress before. I had seen flashes of the demon's existence in his impatience and unreasoning pride. But I had learned how to soothe the beast back into purring submission; how to laugh and smile in defense against imagined crimes; how to wait, caring and patient, for the coals of anger to cool, the embers to give up their reddish heat. I had learned how to be a wife. Suddenly feeling empathy with Kunle, I rushed over to him. His towel had dropped onto the floor and he was naked, tears streaming down his face.

"Femi, Femi, stop, it's enough," I pleaded, my hands gripping the bulging muscles of his broad shoulders.

Exhausted, he stopped. "Now get out!" he shouted to the boy, a trembling heap on the floor. "Get out! I give you five minutes." He stalked into the bedroom and slammed the door. Kunle reached for the towel and I turned away, heartsick for him.

Kunle left with his suitcases. It was a Sunday and all that day Femi was hard as marbles, so I treaded lightly around him. In the evening Jide came to the house with Kunle. Femi refused to allow Kunle into the house, so they stood on the porch. Jide tried to mediate. Kunle's face was puffy and sore and he refused to speak. Femi repeated over and over, "He disrespects me and I will not have him in my house."

"He said he left some things here," Jide finally said, in exasperation. Yetunde brought a box with Kunle's remaining clothes and handed them to Jide. Femi then walked away from his brothers as though they were strangers.

The next week Femi's mother arrived from Ado-Ekiti. News of the estrangement of her sons traveled with mysterious, unexpected speed, rousing her from the calm of her village life and bringing her to Lagos.

Hearing a knock, I opened the front door expecting to see Femi, prepared to ask why he hadn't used his key. Instead I found his mother, chaperoned by one of Bisi's younger sisters. As she stood on the porch before me, her rigid, intractable glance answered the surprise that bloomed instantly in my eyes. I welcomed her, bowing slightly, and took the goatskin bag containing her clothes.

When Femi entered the house half an hour later, he welcomed his mother by prostrating before her in respect, bravely bringing his glance to meet hers despite his uneasiness. After dinner and several hours spent archly trading gossip and news of relatives, Femi's mother voiced her concern. I stood in the kitchen helping Yetunde shell and grind the beans that would be fried into cakes for breakfast the next morning.

"Tell me what happened," she asked Femi in Yoruba, sitting on the edge of her chair as if she feared missing a single word.

"Kunle disrespected me. He is lazy, arrogant and refused to work. He is a child and yet he walked through this house as though he were more man than I."

"And so you beat him?"

"Yes I did. He disrespected me and that he cannot do."

His mother stood up slowly, her eyes bright with rage. "He is your brother and you had no right, no matter what, to beat him. You are my child, he is my child, and as long as I live none of my sons should raise a hand in anger against the other."

"But mama—"

"Quiet! You listen to me," she shouted, silencing him. "Even your father hardly beat any of you. And you, *my son*, Kunle's brother, gave that right to yourself? Did those years in America make you so foolish?" She strutted before Femi, now in front of him, now bearing down over his shoulder with the force of her words, her face, arms, body all emphasizing, driving home her outrage. "You say he disrespects you. If you act in a manner that will earn his respect I am sure it will be yours. But never again do I want to hear of such an act." Pounding her chest, she said, "Strike me before you strike your brother."

"But he must know—" Femi began again.

"There is nothing that he must know that he will not learn in time," she interrupted him. "Yes, you are a man, but before you are a man, Femi, you are my son, and you are the brother of Kunle and Jide. You are part of the Ajayi family, and you make no law unto yourself."

Hoisting her wrapper tighter at her waist, she said, "And my son, you forget that at your own risk." Then she stalked into the back bedroom and closed the door.

As he looked into the kitchen, Femi's sheepish glance caught my eye. His expression was as befuddled as a child's. Going to the back of the apartment, he knocked on the door of the bedroom his mother had been given.

"*Wole*," she said, telling him to enter. I heard the door gently close behind him, and soon I heard their voices as well, alternately soft, mellow, gay, and the sound of laughter soon joined me in the kitchen.

The next evening she sat, satisfied and proud, surrounded by her three sons. Now reunited, their conversation and camaraderie were a burst of sunlight filling up the room. Her task completed, she rose at five-thirty the next morning and headed back to Ado-Ekiti.

August. The rainy season soaked through my skin, leaving my spirit soggy and limp. Since early June I had been on vacation from the university, and the continual downpour pushed me to the edge of an emotional precipice. As I slid toward that edge, only my writing rescued me from a fall. Having completed the first draft of my novel, I longed to have it read. So I went back to the States to wait out the rains, to have my novel read by my mentors, to connect with the friends and family I left behind. As the plane took off, a ball of sickness gathered in the pit of my stomach. I reached for the sick bag just in time. I had never thrown up on takeoff or landing before. Then I realized that I had missed my period.

Manhattan, August 2. Wanda's apartment, a tiny studio crammed with books, plants, a Buddhist *gohonzan* in one corner. The room mirrors her—small, puzzling and peaceful. Borderline jumble, yet the order, the design is clear. The room breathed space. A mountain could fit in here. My mother's plants filled the windows and had bloomed under her hand. Her cat O.J. padded around the room, assessing me as though I were a stranger. George Benson's "Masquerade" played on the stereo. She peeled away the first layer after hugs and kisses, telling me of lovers, work and scripts she was reading. The words turned somersaults, eager and tiptoeing simultaneously. She was a member of a respected theater company and the work was more regular. We hid behind gossip, extraneous complaints, fads and fashions I've missed. Then, finally, we stripped away the bark and exposed the flesh.

"I didn't know if we'd still be friends," she said, a smile attempting to dull the sharpness of her words.

"Why?" I asked. "We've written regularly." I recalled the letters—one a cry for help banged out on her typewriter at 3 A.M., half an hour after the lover who took her to bed but never stayed had gone for the night. My hands shook as I called her the same day I received the letter and found her recovered from an urge to slit her wrists. I recalled the ones, too, where she told me she'd begun keeping a diary, was writing poetry, knew someday she wanted to direct. I kissed the pages of those letters as I felt the rays of her intelligence and will and missed her so much.

"I know," she continued hesitantly, "it's just that—"

"I don't understand. How can you wonder if we'd still be friends?" I badgered her, standing up, hands on hips, as though lecturing a naughty child. I watched her shrink beneath my annoyed glance.

"But you have another life. A new life. With Femi. And I'm not part of it."

"No, you're not. But you're part of me." I stooped before her. "I will always love you. You have to know that. In a way that's

different and more lasting than my love for Femi." She was surprised by this revelation and looked at me as though I had betrayed him. "You are me," I said emphatically. "You'll never fail
me. You are my friend. He is my husband. That love is so condi-
tional, so demanding, and sometimes so tenuous. I'm afraid it
could evaporate in the moment it takes to kiss."

Relieved, she asked, "Are you happy?"

"Yes. I've found what I needed."

August 3. The city has not missed me. Not enough to change its
ways. Went shopping today. Was jostled and pushed and
shoved. For all the backwardness of Lagos, gratefully it lacks the
egocentric desperation of New York. Lagos endures in spite of itself. New York is the nightmare turned into a horror show. No
one dares change the channel. I will never love this city again.

August 4. Went to MOMA and the Whitney today. Getting there
the IRT stalled for half an hour between stations. In Lagos I'd
daydreamed of the convenience of fast mass transportation.
Struggling simply to breathe inside the stifling, airless train, I
felt bitter every time that memory popped into my head. Finally
the train moved. Its steel body groaned and screeched, its voice
bouncing against the tunnel's hollow darkness. "Robert of 110th
Street" emblazoned the windows on both sides in stark blue
spray-painted letters. A young Puerto Rican girl sat biting her
nails, her olive skin mapped with tiny pimples. Her long, ripe
legs poured from a pair of lime-colored hot pants that clenched
her hips.

In a corner sat an old woman, her bloated legs the color of
dying flesh, wrapped in layers of filthy peeling cloth. She rocked
back and forth in her seat. Her anguished, hysterical voice
climbed the hot, stuffy air of the ruined car, rubbing against
each person in turn. The train shuddered into Times Square.
Carrying two bags of newspapers, the old woman rose and
pushed her way out of the car with the finesse of the partial sur-
vivor she was.

August 6. I am pregnant. Today I went to Wanda's gynecologist

in Greenwich Village. She confirmed my suspicion. Her basement office was cool and airy as she moved around the room,
washing her hands, putting on the plastic gloves, gathering the
jelly for a pelvic exam. Her thick German-Jewish accent fluttered
like a butterfly as her hand pushed against my pelvic wall. "Ah
yes. I tink so. Yes. Definitely." Washing her hands at the sink,
she asked, "Do you want to keep the baby?"

I was startled by the question, which more than anything told
me I was in the States. "Yes, of course," I snapped back defensively.

"I did not know," she shrugged, looking at me kindly. "Motherhood is no longer a necessity but an option." She smiled trium-
phantly at her statement.

"Here it is an option," I thought, as I reached for my clothes.

Wanda and I met for lunch at a restaurant on Eighth Avenue.
She leaned over to hug me, nearly knocking over our drinks
when I told her the news. "That's great. How do you feel?"

"I don't know. Most of all I'm simply relieved that it's finally
happened. Now Femi will have his child. But I'm scared too. I
try to imagine what this will mean for me, for the things I want,
and I always see them slipping from my hand. I feel guilty because I still want to just be me for a little while longer. Belong to
just me and Femi before someone else claims me too."

August 11. Had lunch today with my former fiction professor
and mentor Sidney Offit. He had read my manuscript and liked
the first draft, but he said it needed more work and suggested
another possible story line.

August 15. I am battling morning sickness that leaves me emotionally and physically depleted. I can't eat. Have no appetite.
The nausea is a huge iron fist balling into knuckles and bones,
pushing violently against the walls of my stomach. It rises, fills
my chest, contracts my throat, makes me gag. I hold my breath,
praying to reach the bathroom in time. There I retch and retch.
When it is over, I feel as if I've been beaten. In the morning, as
soon as my feet touch the floor, my body is a weathervane, responding to the change in gravity. I begin to sweat, feel the

enemy marshaling forces. Yet it always surprises me. I live in fear of it mugging my ease and confidence. The past three days I have craved, of all things, pounded yam and stew.

August 16. Washington, D.C., back to ghosts. I visited my parents' graves and wondered what they would think of my life. Wondered if I would have *this* life if they were still here. I showed my aunt and uncle pictures of our apartment so they would be assured that we do not live in the bush. I told them about the university. They nodded approval that in no way comprehended my existence. How could it? I did *not* tell them about the blackouts, the water shortages, the coup. Over dinner my uncle asked me what other Africans think about Idi Amin.

August 18. Tonight I watched a talk show. An actress was discussing her former heroin addiction, an author multiple orgasms. Gripped by culture shock, I was offended by the public sharing of experiences so intimate and longed for the modesty and mystery of Nigerian society.

August 21. Back to New York. Went to lunch with a friend today. Had to leave the table in the middle of the meal to throw up.

August 23. Dr. Schwartz gave me a prescription for pills to stop the nausea. Now I vomit less but still have no appetite.

17

The living room floor was littered with my open suitcases and the gifts I had brought back for everyone. I rummaged through my bags, searching out each gift, showing it to Femi for approval. As he stacked the shirts and slacks I brought him on the top of the television set, I finally told him.

"I'm going to have a baby." Instantly his face glowed with happiness and surprise. And just as quickly I was bathed in the knowledge that if I could not give him a child he could never imagine a way to love me. Bitterness welled up, leaving a bad taste in my mouth at this thought.

"Now we'll be a real family," he said, reaching for me, gazing curiously at my stomach.

"It's due in March." I smiled falsely as I turned over and over in my head his words "Now we'll be a real family" and disputed within myself his conclusion that our childless existence had been fraudulent.

"We'll have a large naming ceremony," he said, standing up to pace the floor like a landowner reveling in his wealth. "My mother will come." I slumped back into the chair and thought of the second draft of my novel. I'd wanted to begin it in the three weeks before school began. I wondered if I could. "You look tired," he observed. "Go on to bed. Let Yetunde put your things away." He helped me into the bedroom as though I were already heavy with child. As he walked out of the room, the last thing I heard him say was, "It will be a boy. I know it."

As he awaited the birth of his child, his son, Femi's happiness was a badge proudly worn. It checked his impatience, quelled his temper and turned his hands into loving shelters. When I rose from the table, running to the bathroom, my stomach plotting an uprising, his face creased with worry. Finished, I opened the bathroom door to find him standing at the end of the hall. He rushed forward to help me back to the table. The smell of nearly everything—palm oil, plantains, stew—made me sick and he worried over me. I assured him the nausea wouldn't last much longer and wrapped myself tighter in the blanket of concern he offered. He made love to me as though I were made of finely cut glass, and he became vulnerable and wondering, like me, like the child I carried. The armor of strength lay on the floor. He would fit it round his shoulders in the morning.

October, and the dry season descended. The day awoke, flushed and humid. By noon the sun had parched the city into willing acceptance of its dominance. Three o'clock and the landscape was scorched by blistering rays that would turn into a moon patrolling a sultry, sticky night.

One afternoon I drove by Femi's office on my way home. The secretary who manned a small desk in the foyer was nowhere around. As I walked toward Femi's office, I heard the bathroom door open and Boye, the messenger, came toward me. "Hello, madam," he greeted me.

"Hello, Boye. Is my husband here?"

"No, madam. He went to the mainland but said he would be back by two-thirty."

I glanced at my watch. It was one o'clock. "I haven't time to wait. I'll leave a note on his desk," I said. When I entered Femi's office, I found his partner Olu Akinyemi gazing out the window at the traffic-filled street. I had never liked him. Where Femi saw ambition and confidence, I saw arrogance. He displayed his affluence with more than the usual Nigerian talent for ostentatiousness. He collected mistresses like cars. And more than once he had reminded Femi how much he'd done for him. When I entered the room, he turned, showing little surprise to find me rather than Femi.

"Mrs. Ajayi," he said as he strode forward, offering his hand. "How are you? Long time, long time," he said jovially.

"I'm fine," I said, sitting down at Femi's desk. "I just want to leave a note for Femi," I said, and began writing a message. Akinyemi stood beside me, leaning over my shoulder, peering at what I was writing, when suddenly I felt his palm rubbing the small of my back. "Mr. Akinyemi, please stop that."

"What, Mrs. Ajayi?" he asked innocently.

"What you're doing." I sat up straight, composing my face into an expression of sternness that I hoped would hide my panic.

He moved his hand, grinning. "Alright." I looked up at him and his glance hit me like a naked bulb in an interrogation room. "It's just that I thought you might enjoy a massage."

"Why?"

"Femi tells me you're going to have a baby." He emitted the words slowly. They were brutish hands ripping open my blouse. I imagined buttons rolling across the floor.

"I didn't know my health was your concern."

"Children concern us all in Africa," he said, smiling slyly. Gathering the robes of his *agbada*, he sat on the desk. I continued to write the note, tearing it from the pad and folding it neatly. When I looked at him again, preparing a curt good-bye in my mind, he said, "I want you. You've known that for a long time, haven't you?" My body weighed a ton from the shoulders down and I wondered how I would stand up and walk away. "You're an attractive woman," he continued with vehemence and

a hint of impatience. I thought perhaps if I willed my energy into
my feet the leaden feeling would leave and I could push the
chair back and stand up. He slid closer to me, and his voice
lowered, his hand preparing to touch me. I wondered how it
would arrive. Grab all of a sudden to frighten? Waltz onto my
shoulders? Take me unawares? Gripping the table, I pushed myself back and in an instant he was before me, shoving me back
into the chair. I thought how I detest disorder, clutter, unmade
beds, dirty plates in the sink, cigarette butts. How would I put
myself back in order after today? "You don't have to make up
your mind now," he pleaded. "But just consider it. We've plenty
of time. Think carefully." He touched my arm. His hands were
large and, I noticed for the first time, ugly. Scarred, calloused
and dry, the nails were black with dirt.

"Olu, please let me leave," I begged.

"Alright," he sighed, his voice a white flag. But he did not
move. His hands journeyed to my face and he leaned forward to
kiss me. His lips threatened to touch mine and I slapped him,
then pushed him away with arms strengthened by anger. "Don't
worry, I won't rape you," he jeered from the floor.

"I'm not one of your mistresses. I don't need your money or
your goodwill." He began to laugh so loudly, so hard that Boye
came in from the hallway. Puzzled, he looked at us both. Olu
laughed demoniacally as I ran to the door, rushed down the hall,
heading for the bathroom.

Breathlessly, I searched my face in the mirror for a hint of in-
cendiary intent. Yet what I saw was the face I had spent a year
shaping. It was complacent, predictable. It was what I had determined a married woman's face should be. I belonged to Femi
and shunned the burden of flirtations, extraneous sexual attrac-
tions, finding even their suggestion offensive and frightening. For
they would rip me from the womb. And I gestated as surely as
the child within me then.

We were the last ones to arrive for Sara's dinner party. A born
hostess, she used any excuse to have guests; tonight it was a celebration of Thanksgiving. As Femi and I entered the living room,
I saw Anita sitting on the sofa, dressed in a long lavender caftan,

a jade necklace and matching earrings. I introduced Femi and she presented her husband Banji.

As she gripped a drink with one hand, her eyes patrolled the room as though she were preparing for some kind of assault. Despite the smartly tailored safari suit he wore, her husband was ordinary, even nondescript in appearance. Several inches shorter than she, he wore thick bifocals and peered uncertainly at whatever was before him. The beginnings of a beard tufted his chin and cheeks and he self-consciously rubbed his face.

"How've you been?" she asked as I sat beside her.

"Okay."

"How far along are you now?"

"Five months."

"Halfway," she said quietly, looking down at her drink.

"What did you decide about your job?"

"I'm still there. Teaching art to all those brats at the American International School." She laughed, pure and untroubled for a moment.

I touched that equilibrium, tried to hold on to it. "But the salary's great, I hear."

"It's good," she admitted. "In fact, it's very good. Enough for me to go home every summer and spend it all on clothes, shoes, makeup and jewelry. Isn't that right, Banji?" Her voice careened near the edge again.

"What?" he asked, turning from a conversation with Femi.

"Nothing. Banji says no woman needs all the clothes I have. He tells me I'm overcompensating for something. I asked him for what, but he won't tell me." She threw her head back and drained the glass.

"Have you done any more painting?" I ventured.

"A little. You have to be in a certain mood to create. There has to be a will present that right now I just don't have."

"I haven't written a word since I got pregnant," I confessed. "I just don't have the energy. For a long time what I was writing was my center, a fix that kept me sane and helped me make sense of things."

"Painting was a kind of glue for me too," she said, her eyes connecting with mine the way her laugh stood straight and tall

moments before. "Then things just came undone. I'm looking for
the pieces but I can't find some of them, and the picture I make
is just a puzzle." She leaned forward, nodding urgently, "You
can understand, can't you?"

"Understand what?" Sara asked loudly, interrupting and shep-
herding us into the conversation with the others. "Another
drink, Anita?" she asked.

"Oh, it's empty. Yes, Sara, I'd like that."

Marian Ogun shouted across the room at me, "You went to the
States recently, I understand." She was a frumpish English-
woman of infinite kindness.

"Actually, I wasn't impressed," I said, walking over to her.
Her husband, Lateef, sat beside her, listening for inconsistencies,
foolish remarks, anything that he could mock, reducing her to a
scarlet-faced windup toy mouthing apologies the rest of the evening. "I mean, I'd forgotten how dirty and unmanageable New
York is. And I actually began to crave yam and stew one day
while I was eating at McDonald's."

This reduced her to raucous laughter. Worried, she shot a
glance at her husband. "We go to England every year and stay
with my parents in the country. It's wonderful. We find the trips
just like a tonic. Isn't that right, Lateef?"

"Yes, Marian," he assured her. Then he sabotaged her assertion by saying, "But the cost of everything in Britain is so high
these days, it's hardly worth it to go anymore."

Her head bobbed up and down in agreement. "He's absolutely
right. Why, I was amazed myself at the cost of things this last
trip."

Before our eyes Sara doted on our husbands with so much
charm and ease that only the initiated suspected the covert nature of her actions. In a sense all our husbands belonged to her.
Her total acquiescence to their culture was enough to steal them
from us. And in this acquiescence she partially relieved us of the
necessity to do it. We envied and despised her ability to enchant
them—flirting in Yoruba, never voicing complaint. Still, we were
powerless to defeat her allure or undermine the allegiance our
husbands unknowingly swore to her. In one corner Wole, Sara's
husband, Banji and Femi argued over the latest government de-

cree banning certain imported items. While putting the finishing touches to the dinner table with her house girl's help, Sara tossed comments into the living room like darts, fueling waning conversation and ever reminding us of her presence. Sara was the woman all our husbands wanted us to be. And because of this desire we vowed to aggressively cherish everything we were that she was not.

Over dessert Anita raised her third scotch and soda, quieting the hum of conversation as she announced, "I'd like to propose a toast." She had been ominously quiet throughout dinner. The intimacy we shared on the sofa had evaporated, leaving me wondering if I imagined it. Now she looked around the table at each of us, her glass held high. Banji removed his glasses and massaged the bridge of his nose. We each picked up our wineglass. Banji picked his up last. "To my husband," she said, looking hard at us as though we were co-conspirators in a heinous crime. A stricken look passed like a flash of thunder over Banji's face. "Congratulations on the birth of his new son. The third son, delivered last night by his second wife." She paused and said, "My *iyawo*," using the Yoruba term for wife.

"Shut up, Anita," Banji hissed.

"Why?" she asked, watching us set our glasses down. "I think it's wonderful. Doesn't everyone else?" Her display chastened us into fidgeting silence. "Well, then, I'll drink the toast by myself," she concluded in a voice sincerely confused. "Here's to Banji and—"

Banji jumped from his chair, wrestled the glass from her hand and tossed the drink in her face. "You foolish woman. You utterly foolish woman. So you're a martyr and I'm a villain. Well I'm not!" he shouted, grabbing her by the neck and beginning to choke her. Femi and Wole sprang from their seats and pulled him off of her. Anita sat on the floor, her face and hair wet, and from the floor she looked up at us, relieved, defiant and sad. Sara, Marian and I led her into the bedroom. Silently Sara wiped her face and hair.

Marian paced the room, mumbling comforting words in a nervous stream. "Anita, it'll be alright. You know Banji loves you." Submitting totally to our attention, Anita sat maniacally twisting the wedding band on her finger. Sara knelt before her, combing her hair, asking sternly, "Do you really think that was fair to Banji?"

In response Anita looked up, her face unnerving in its tranquillity. Her eyes had retreated into remembrance and her voice was as hollow as a wind whipping across the heart of a frozen winter night. "The night my mother took me to the doctor to have it done it was snowing," she said, her eyes narrowing with the effort to remember, then widening again. "We'd taken the train out to Flatbush and he lived several long blocks from the station." She touched her face and smiled. "The snow felt like cotton against my lips and cheeks, sticking to it, then melting all of a sudden. Mama was walking real fast, almost like she didn't want anybody to know we were together. I kept calling to her, asking her to slow down, to wait for me. All I could see was her back hunched over against the cold, while she walked fast and steady against the snow. I started running and finally I caught up with her and said, 'Mama, don't leave me.' She looked at me just like she didn't know who I was. Then she shook her head and started throwing words at me like rocks, calling me fast and no good. Then she said, 'Lord, I hope you'll forgive me for this mission I'm on tonight.' She stopped in the middle of the street and looked up at the sky and threw her arms out and said in a whisper I could hardly hear, 'Lord, forgive me.' Then she put her hands in her pockets and walked ahead of me just like before. She didn't look at me anymore that night. Not when the doctor made me lie on the table and stuck the catheter inside of me. Not even when the pain got so bad I felt like my skin was peeling away and my womb was on fire. I was wishing I'd die and I started screaming and the doctor opened the door and told her to make me be quiet. But she wouldn't look at me. I could see her sitting in a corner of the room in a folding chair. She sat there, huddled against me and what was happening just like she'd been huddled against the snow. No, she didn't look at me. Not even after it was over and there was blood everywhere and the doctor had to carry me downstairs behind my mama and hold me in his arms till the taxi came, 'cause I was too weak to stand by myself. She never looked at me for a long time after that night. Eyes just ran away whenever my look came near. Now when I look at Banji his eyes run away too." Marian clicked her tongue and shook her head. "He doesn't see me now, just like she wouldn't see me then."

"Your mama wouldn't look at you because she was afraid she'd see a murderer reflected in your eyes," I said gently. "Banji can't look at you because he's ashamed and afraid to be proud of his sons."

"It's nobody's fault," Marian offered, "not yours, not Banji's."

Sara moved from the bureau, where she had stood listening with her back to us. Arms folded across her chest she gazed contemptuously at Anita. "Your barrenness could've made you useless to him. Don't you know that? As useless as someone deaf, dumb and blind," she said impatiently. "If he'd left you, no one in this society would have blamed him. Did you ever ask why he didn't leave? Why he didn't just do what the Yorubas used to do to twins—take them into the forest and leave them there to die because they were thought to be cursed? If you don't pull yourself together, he will leave you, since you can't leave him. He must look at you now and wonder where you are, behind your tears and self-pity. You can't give him a child. At least give him someone to respect and maybe love again.

"I'm going to finish my dessert," she announced icily. The door slammed hard behind her, leaving the three of us chafed and speechless, clinging to each other in confusion. Moments later her voice, soothing and apologetic, floated into the bedroom from the dining room where our husbands sat, seduced into good humor by her reassuring presence.

The nurse shook her head in dismay. "This will not do. This will not do," she said, looking at the small spot of blood she had taken from my finger. She shot most of it into a vial and tested one spot. "Mrs. Ajayi, your iron count is very, very low." She paused, then pursed her lips in disgust. "Are you eating at all?"

"I have no appetite. I'm tired all the time."

"You *must* think of the baby. You must force yourself to eat," she admonished me in her displeasure. "I want you to eat a slice of liver three or four times a week, and I'm going to give you a series of liver injections to bring your iron count up," she warned me, as though I had failed a crucial exam.

The fetus was gobbling me whole. Since my return from New York I had not written a single page. Writing was the only child I wanted then, and I was racked by a sense of guilt because of my inability to nurture it. Finally, one afternoon, buoyed by a sudden resolve and determination, I entered my study and sat down at my desk. Staring at the legal-size yellow pad, I felt the characters tiptoe around the edge of my brain, but within half an hour I had slumped into a deep, unremitting slumber. I woke three hours later, my cheek glued to the naked page by a pool of saliva, the room filled with early-evening shadows.

After each class at school I collapsed in my office, whipped by fatigue. Evenings I fell into bed moments after I entered the house. Most nights Femi arrived to find me already asleep.

I stumbled through my life like a zombie. My body had turned on me, become my enemy. Thoughts of the child I carried evoked resentment and fear. I dared not give voice to my secret: How dare I become a mother when it was I who was still a child?

Two weeks after the liver injections were completed, I developed a yeast infection and was given two weeks' worth of large bullet-shaped suppositories to cure it.

"But I read somewhere that you shouldn't use suppositories when you're pregnant," I protested to Dr. Sonaike.

Standing with his back to me as he wrote out the prescription, he said, "Mrs. Ajayi, I would not give you anything that wasn't safe to use." Turning to me, he reached over his desk and took my hand, leading me condescendingly to the door.

Calamities trailed me. Three weeks later I slipped in the parking lot at school, scraped my knee and had to undergo a series of penicillin injections to prevent infection. I was uneasy. In Nigeria the injection is the cure-all, as the pill is in the United States. I wondered about my child, how it could withstand such an onslaught of medication, which I knew must find its way into its watery home.

As his own boss, Femi was dissatisfied with the progress of his business. While he had designed numerous small projects—a high school in Ikorodu, a block of apartments, and a modern clinic, all financed by the federal government, he had yet to find a sponsor for his grander designs—like a self-contained seventy-five-unit apartment complex that would include a shopping mall and school. His days were long and often he did not get home until eight or nine at night. He was nearly frantic, worried that he would not have enough money for the elaborate naming ceremony and party he wanted for our child. While I reminded him that it takes time for a new business to take off, he was more comfortable believing he was unlucky or incompetent. He wondered aloud to his brother Jide, "Has someone put a curse on me?" He was stalking a lodestone of wealth and feared he would never find it.

18

I began losing the baby a week before Christmas. For two days I'd released a heavy, whitish discharge. It had not frightened me, for I thought it was merely a recurrence of the yeast infection. Now, as I stood up to flush the toilet, I saw a thin stream of dark red blood curdling inside the toilet bowl. Stuffing a wad of toilet paper between my legs, I pulled on my panties. Femi was taking a nap on the sofa. I kneeled on the floor beside him, trying to remain calm, but when he sleepily opened his eyes I gave in to panic and tears, blurting out, "Femi, I'm bleeding. I think I'm losing the baby."

It was a Sunday afternoon and the clinic was nearly deserted. Terrified by visions of delivering my child while stalled in traffic on the way to the mainland, I'd registered at the clinic months before because it was near our house and Sara had recommended it highly. A nurse sat in the dispensary window idly thumbing through a newspaper. She told us that Dr. Sonaike, who lived in a spacious house next door to the clinic, was out of town and wouldn't be back until the next day.

"Well, who can I see? I must see someone. I'm hemorrhaging," I insisted. Dr. Sonaike's assistant, whom I had never met, came into the hallway. I explained what was happening, how I felt.

"You'll have to stay off your feet completely the next several days. Don't do anything. Don't go to work," he said, and began writing a prescription, which he handed to the nurse in the dispensary. "I'm giving you some pills that will stop the bleeding," he assured me, patting my hand and looking at Femi.

"But why am I bleeding? Is the baby coming?"

"The main thing is not to worry. Relax and stay in bed. Check back with us in a few days." With those instructions he turned and walked away, completely dismissing my anxiety.

"You see, it's not so serious," Femi said. But I was offended by the doctor's quick dismissal of my apprehension and could not forget the blood in the toilet bowl.

At home I took a tablet and got into bed. For several hours I slept peacefully, then a spasm of severe contractions in my back and stomach yanked me from sleep. The contractions were like red-hot wires pressed against my muscles, traveling irregularly in short spurts and long convulsions. I lay in the bed, realizing that the baby was not just kicking or shifting position but trying to leave my womb, making its journey out of me at the end of six months. I sat up in bed, snapped on the light and called Yetunde.

"Ma?" she asked, entering the room.

"Tell Femi to please come." As he sat on the bed beside me, a contraction traveled around my waist. I held my breath to keep from screaming. "Femi, it's worse. Now I'm having pains as well."

He looked at me as though determined *not* to believe me. "But why? Did you take the pills?" he asked skeptically.

"Yes, you know I did. You saw me take them."

Pulling back the sheet and slipping his hand under my gown, he asked, "Where is the pain?"

"In my back and stomach."

His hand was cool against the warm skin of my belly. He left his palm on my stomach for a long time and then said, "I don't feel anything."

"It comes and goes."

"We'll have to go back to the clinic," he concluded.

He drove slowly this time, carefully dodging the potholes and craters that filled the road. I clung to the door handles, trying to absorb the shock of the jarring movements of the car. At the clinic the young doctor looked at us in surprise when he saw us enter. In apologetic tones that attempted to undermine the seriousness of what was happening, Femi told him about the pains. The doctor took me into his office and examined me. As I lay on the table, he shook his head. Leaning on his hands, he looked down at me.

"You should be in a hospital. But we have no empty beds, We're full."

Sitting up, I shouted, "I'm registered with this clinic, am losing my baby, and you're telling me you have no room for me?"

"I'd refer you to the clinic, but no doubt there are no empty beds there either. The only thing I can tell you is to go back home, stay off your feet and continue to take the pills."

"Will the pills stop the contractions?"

"Yes. But it's important that you relax."

"How can I relax with what's happening to me?" I screamed.

"You see, this is what I mean," he pointed out. "You must stay calm and that way the pills will ease the contractions."

"When can I see Dr. Sonaike?"

"He'll be back tomorrow. I will tell him you were here." As I started to dress, alone in the room, I began to cry, feeling my life and my child's endangered.

As we prepared to leave, the doctor conferred with Femi. In the car Femi said, "The doctor feels that these pains may be your imagination."

"My imagination?"

"Yes. You must do exactly as he told you," he ordered, "unless you want to lose the baby."

"Femi, this pain is real. Believe me. The blood is real. You saw it."

He began driving not just to dodge potholes but to release his
anger as well, and I saw the fear on his face that I felt inside.
When we arrived home, he slammed his door shut and left me in
the car alone. "If you lose this baby it's your fault," he charged,
as I passed him on the way to the bedroom, leaning on Yetunde.

As soon as my back touched the bed, the contractions began,
tremors splitting my body, cracking open my womb into a throb-
bing crater. In the dark I imagined the baby, its fists punching
through the shell of water, mucus and blood, bursting out to
freedom and killing me in the process. The pain was everywhere,
traveling to my temples and settling into a migraine. I turned on
the light and sat up, which eased but did not dissipate the pain.
Suddenly hot, I stripped naked and paced the bedroom floor,
clutching my back and stomach. Femi came into the room and
held me to him. Suffocating and hot, I worked my way out of his
arms.

"I can't sit still, I can't lie down. I'm hot, I'm tired," I moaned.

"He said you wouldn't lose it if you stayed in bed," he whim-
pered.

"I can't lie down, Femi. I can't. The pain is much worse then."

He massaged my back, gave me more pills, raged that I
wouldn't get into bed. I never had seen him so helpless or so lost.
"You must get back into bed," he insisted.

"If I lie down, I'll just get up again," I snapped, as a tight-
fisted contraction plowed across my back and stomach. Swirling,
I began falling to the floor. Femi caught me and laid me on the
bed. Only half conscious, I lay twisting inside the sheets, holding
my breath, sobbing and screaming. "Yetunde," he called. "Run
to my brother's house. Tell him to come."

Jide and Bisi arrived and I barely heard their voices. I could
not see them because the pain did not allow me to open my eyes.
A few minutes later I heard the controlled and authoritative
voice of the woman who lived next door to us. Her hand was on
my forehead as she called, "Marita, Marita, can you hear me?"

"Yes," I whispered.

"My dear, we're taking you to the hospital. You will be
alright." I was lifted onto a stretcher and put in an ambulance.

The pains began to subside and the last face I saw before blacking out was Femi's.

I remained at the army hospital all the next day, and there the injections to stop the contractions began. Femi came to see me on his way to work. "Thank God you are well. I was afraid I was going to lose you. Later today they will take you to the clinic. I'm going there now to talk to Dr. Sonaike."

That evening Dr. Sonaike explained what was happening. "You are having a spontaneous abortion. We are going to do all we can to stop the baby from dilating your cervix. The more contractions, the more your cervix dilates and the closer the fetus is to being expelled from the womb. We'll be giving you injections to stop the contractions. If the pain gets very bad, push this buzzer"—he pointed to a buzzer hanging from a cord on the wall —"and a nurse will come. I will check on you every day."

I was calmed by the gentleness in his eyes, for in them was a softness that replenished me. "Now, at least, I know what is happening," I said. "But what about the baby's will?"

"What do you mean?"

"You assume the injections will stop its push downward, its attempts to leave my body. But I feel as though some process has begun that is resistant to my prayers and your medication."

"Is that your woman's intuition?"

"Yes."

"Discard it this time, Mrs. Ajayi. I won't let you lose this baby."

In the evenings I was visited by Femi, Jide, Bisi, Sara, Anita—even Kunle. The pains occurred throughout the day and night, and soon my body was sore from injections. I had so many injections in my hips that by the third day the nurse had to give them to me in my thighs. It was Christmastime and Dr. Sonaike's wife had decorated a tree in the main entrance. At night the sound of Christmas carols gently wafted through the halls from a record player in the front office. One night a power failure threw the entire area into darkness. My room was lit, like the others, by candles. I had had a relatively good day, with little pain, and began to think that the injections would work. But that night the pain recurred, more virulent than ever. I rang the buzzer and the

nurse came. Her shadow loomed ghostlike against the wall and
the candle on the table flickered nervously.

"What is it, Mrs. Ajayi?"

"The pain is starting again."

"But I just gave you an injection an hour ago."

"I know," I said, embarrassed and near tears because of the
accusing tone of her voice, "but it's back." She left the room and
returned armed with the hypodermic needle that I no longer
feared, that had become my friend. She pulled back the sheets
and another nurse held a kerosene lamp over her shoulder so
that she could find a vein in my thigh. "Thank you," I whispered,
while the needle of the third injection in five hours punctured
skin and muscles. When she left the pain subsided for what
seemed only a moment and then started again. I reached for the
buzzer and pressed it repeatedly, but no one came. After raging
for what seemed an eternity, the pain subsided and finally I fell
asleep.

Christmas day, after Femi left, Sara arrived. She bounded into
the room with a picnic basket covered with a red-checked tea
towel. "What's this?" I asked, sitting up.

"Your Christmas dinner. Since you can't come for the dinner
party tonight, I brought it to you," she explained while examining
me closely. Her hands rummaged through my hair, which was
matted and dry, unkempt and uncombed. "How do you feel?"

"Right now, I'd give anything for a bath."

"Let me take care of that." She rang the buzzer. A young
nurse's aide came in and she ordered her to bring a bucket of
water and clean towels.

"They told me to stay off my feet," I explained, suddenly
aware of my own body odor.

"It's not your fault. It's the nurse's job to bathe patients." The
girl brought the water and Sara told her to put it on the table.
Propping me up on the thick pillows, she removed my gown.
Swiftly her hands took charge, momentarily relieving me of the
sorrow congealed inside the marrow of my bones. Closing my
eyes, I gave myself up to her touch, as the sponge, lathered and
cool, slid over my skin. Lovingly her hands washed my body.
Gently she wiped the mound of my stomach. Expertly she

washed me down to my toes, then patted my skin dry with the skimpy clinic towel. Finishing up, she massaged lotion into my arms, legs and shoulders.

The picnic basket she had brought was a treasure chest of delights—turkey, dressing, sweet potatoes, gravy, stringbeans, rolls and cranberry sauce. "Sara, I don't believe this."

"What, the cranberry sauce? I stocked up on it once I heard the government was going to ban it."

"Yeah," I laughed, "the cranberry sauce." I gazed at the food, almost afraid to touch it.

"Go on, eat," she ordered, sitting at the foot of the bed to watch me.

Over the tinkling of dishes being placed back in the basket, to draw her attention, I said, "I didn't want this baby." I sat staring at my hands, fumbling with the china cup she had brought and filled with coffee from a thermos. "I didn't want it," I said again and then looked at her, "but I didn't want to lose it. Not like this. I didn't want it to die."

She looked at me, retreating, somehow denying the understanding I had sought. "You haven't lost the baby. And you won't," she said, pat and sure.

"But that's not what I'm talking about, Sara. There were times when I hated it because it made me weak and tired, and people looked at me and saw only my stomach, and the me I hardly even knew disappeared behind the shadow the baby cast. I hated it, Sara. But I didn't want it to die."

"Stop talking as if you've lost it," she demanded.

"I heard Dr. Sonaike tell the nurse yesterday my cervix is now three fingers wide. That was yesterday. Two more fingers and the baby can come out."

Talking more to herself than to me, she said, "I'm happiest when I'm pregnant. So everyone I love becomes, in a way, a child for me. And the children I have, I worry over them and love them and they rebel against me, grow up and away from me. And one day they will leave me alone. What will I do then? Anyway," she said slowly, gathering her composure, "Merry Christmas." Kissing me on the forehead, she said, "I'll be back tomorrow."

"Thank you, Sara. Thank you," I said.

"For what?" she asked.

"For everything."

The next afternoon Dr. Sonaike examined me. Dismayed, he said, "Your cervix is five fingers wide, Mrs. Ajayi. Your baby is nearly ready to be delivered. I will have to take it out."

Before I could react, with the help of a nurse he moved me into a portable chair and wheeled me into the delivery room. The nurse helped me onto the cushioned table while Dr. Sonaike put on his gloves. Within seconds he parted my thighs and his hand burrowed into my vagina. In one clean, quick grasp the fetus was removed. My stomach was choking, and for an instant —during which I confronted, almost accidentally, my own death —I heard my screams released from inside my womb and inside my heart. "Oh, God. Oh, God. Oh, oh, oh, oh, oh, Goddddddddddddddddddd." The words beat inside my brain in time with the pain ravaging me. As I shivered on the hard metal table, Dr. Sonaike examined the fetus. "Mrs. Ajayi, I'm sorry," he said apologetically, "your baby is dead."

Watching him leave the room and call the nurse, I felt nothing. Nothing except an emptiness as vast as death itself must be. I lay still, no longer trembling, my body plundered, my soul laid to waste. I let the emptiness wash over me, wishing it would seal my eyes and numb my brain forever.

That evening Femi came, and when he entered the room I sat up and stretched my arms out to him. "I'm sorry. I'm so sorry," I sobbed into his chest.

"Don't worry. I didn't want to lose you. Through all of this I was most afraid of losing you."

At home I recuperated, confined by the doctor, Femi and my own desire to bed. Almost immediately I began to write furiously, with the fervor of a long-awaited eruption. I filled page after page with an outpouring the loss of my child released. The writing affirmed me, anointed me with a sense of purpose. Most of all, it slowly began to dissipate the sense of failure that squatted, a mannerless intruder, inside my spirit. The writing redeemed my talent for creation and, as the days passed, made me whole once again.

In the evenings Bisi came to visit, and for several days under her hand I received a postpartum "native treatment." Filling the tub with warm water and an assortment of leaves, grasses and herbs, her hands pressed and gently kneaded my stomach in a downward motion. "This will bring out the poisons," she explained. The water was the color of strong tea and the steam rising from it made me drowsy. Drying me with a towel, she warned, "Tell uncle to let you rest. Let your body heal. Tell him to be patient."

"I will," I assured her, "I will."

Mourning the loss of his child, his son, Femi inhabited the house with me but was dazed with grief. As I ate dinner from a tray in bed one evening, he said, "We lost a man."

"No, Femi, we lost a child."

"We lost my son," he insisted. "And we must find out why this happened. What went wrong, so that it won't happen again. Next time you will not drive; the roads alone could cause a miscarriage."

"Femi, the doctor told me that sometimes a weak or defective fetus will spontaneously abort. That perhaps if that child had gone nine months, it may not have been a healthy baby anyway."

In response he quieted me with a wave of his hand. "We will be more careful next time."

19

After three weeks I returned to the university in time for the beginning of the second semester. Riding out the storm of convalescence and grief honed some once rough-edged part of me, released some resource I'd unconsciously hoarded. I taught with more confidence, gave more of myself and received a bounty of friendships. One of those friendships was with a twenty-eight-year-old mother of five, who was studying for her law degree. She entered the university after the birth of her fifth child. And with her husband's support, she lived on campus during the week to give more time to her studies. Gratified by her excellent grades, her pride was undermined, however, by guilt at having stepped out of the role of full-time wife and mother. When she went home on the weekends, she relieved her mother-in-law, who cared for the children in her absence, savoring this time with her family. But the night before her departure for the campus, the children threw violent tantrums, begging her to stay. Increasingly she feared ambition had made her selfish.

Weighing the needs of husband and family against her own desires, she found neither camp fulfilled. The oldest in a family of nine children, her father doted on her and instilled in her a sense of independence. A learned, farsighted man, he gave permission for her to marry only on the condition that her husband allow her to go to college when she desired. Once shy, she now confidently entered class discussions and challenged fellow students and teachers. But, more importantly, her expectations of herself and her life had changed radically. In exasperation she said to me one afternoon, "Before I was happy, you know, to be just a wife and mother. Now I want to take holidays. I want to buy nice things. I want a career." In angry self-defense, her husband now regretted his decision to allow her to study, accusing her of neglecting him and the children. After one weekend trip home, she told me, "Saturday morning I was going through our closet and folding up some of the children's old clothes that are too small. I began throwing them in the dustbin. My husband asked what I was doing. I told him we wouldn't be needing them anymore. He pushed me aside and picked the clothes out of the trash, saying, 'Yes we will.'" And though she was normally placid, her voice trembled as she concluded, "I don't want another child and, honestly, I don't know what to do." She was an African woman holding fast to dreams I thought only I had. She protested to no one in particular, "I love my husband, I love my children."

"You didn't count on one day loving yourself as well, did you?" I asked.

"My father prepared me for the possibility," she said, shaking her head. "But he did not tell me the price I would have to pay."

Near the end of the term I suggested to Dr. Opubor, the chairman of the department, the idea of hosting a panel discussion on the relevance of women's liberation to Nigerian women. The winds of change that were challenging women's traditional roles in the West had arrived in Nigeria, overturning age-old assumptions and beliefs. Magazines, newspapers, television talk shows—

all mirrored the arrival of this "unsettling" proposition on African soil. Yet the discussions therein were largely superficial or blatantly emotional. I was curious to know what thoughtful female observers had to say. Was the ideology merely a transported fad, like permanents and soul music, or did it genuinely speak to the needs of Nigerian women, regardless of tribe or status? I put together a panel of three women, accomplished and respected in their fields.

Etta Ibok was a militantly outspoken feminist and journalist for the *Daily Times*. A slender young Igbo woman sporting a close-cropped Afro, she impressed me with her sassiness and drive. Her weekly "Feminine Forum" column in the Sunday *Times* had earned her a large following because of her acerbic wit and her penchant for attacking sacred sex-role cows. Dr. Jade Akande was a member of the law faculty at the university who had spent several years researching and writing on the role of Nigerian women in politics and history. Chief Janet Akinrinade was campaigning for a seat in the constituent assembly that would charter the nation's return to civilian rule.

For the forum the auditorium was packed with students and faculty. I moderated the discussion, and the panel spoke eloquently of tribal laws and customs that oppressed and restricted women, of attitudes that demanded change, of physical labor that turned women into chattel. Chief Akinrinade, a farmer as well as a politician, described the lives of rural women, saying, "They are the silent sufferers, working and bearing children and little more. And the men oppress them so much. They may have as many as four wives but be able to provide for only one. And so the four women are wretched in the house. If he is a farmer, he takes them to the farm, all four of them. The one that deserves beating, he will beat her, and the one that deserves bearing children, she will have them. These women are oppressed and used."

When I asked the panel if African women were oppressed, Dr. Akande spoke like the lawyer she was, saying, "The point is that when you say oppressed, it connotes a lot of things. Oppressed by way of being overused; oppressed by way of being ill-treated; oppressed by way of being maltreated; oppressed by way of being discriminated against. But whichever way you do look at it, there is a section of women that qualifies for that description."

Etta, the journalist, charged, "The society does not think of me as Etta, or Mrs. Akinrinade or Dr. Akande as individuals. We are thought of entirely in the context of the role society has created for us. We are stereotyped, and society does not expect anything from us out of the ordinary or outside that traditional role."

During the question-and-answer period that followed the discussion, the male students bristled with indignation at the women's charges. The female students smiled or groaned openly in recognition of the realities the women uncovered.

It was the same back I had loved for more than four years. After two years in Nigeria, the back was hard and tense, its muscles and skin seeming to resist my hands, to fight against me as I gently stroked and carefully kneaded. Femi's back was like his face—flabby from the comforts of married life yet toughened by the defeats of his career. He took the stalemate of his dreams as a personal affront, a hammerblow aimed only at him.

"That's enough," he said in a muffled, tired voice.

I wiped my lightly oiled palms on a towel and sat on the bed. I wanted to talk to him before he went to sleep. "Femi, what's happening to our money?" I asked, straining to soften the words.

"What do you mean?" His back was still to me, yet I saw it stiffening in defense.

"We just never seem to have any anymore." He turned on his back and looked at the ceiling. "We've split the household bills in half, yet my half seems to be increasing more and more these days."

"You know I'm just managing to keep my head above water with the company. By the time I pay the staff, I've just enough left to pay the rent and buy gasoline for the car."

"I know. But we used to have money for extras," I said, remembering that it had been months since we had gone to a movie or out to dinner. That it had been, in fact, a year since we had gone out any place special. Not since my birthday. "I know and understand that," I said. "But we're running as fast as we used to and going backward. What's happened?"

"A couple of months ago the family meeting decided that my monthly contribution should be larger because we have no children."

"And what did you say?" I exploded.

"What could I say? They're my family."

"I'm your family too. At this rate, we'll never have enough saved to have a child," I said, feeling his loyalty to me, the child we would have one day, undermined.

The last Sunday of every month he and his brother Jide attended the family meeting, a gathering of all the Ajayis living in Lagos. The discussion at the meetings ranged from the behavior of family members—the activities of an unfaithful wife or husband reported to the clan—to a younger member requiring school fees to continue education, or to mediating disputes within the group. The meetings were off limits to me and, significantly, were never held at our house. The family meeting was the parliament of the extended family and, like any parliament, exercised broad powers. Members were assigned a fee to pay each month to support family projects and needs.

"What do you want me to do?" he shouted.

"Why couldn't you simply say no? Tell them that we have bills, we have plans."

"Because I cannot say that. *Oyingbo* wife or no, I cannot say no to my family."

"But you can say no to me," I charged, remembering my requests for extra money to buy things needed in the house, and his plea of poverty. The remembered disappointment rose like a flare. "Always you can say no to me. And always your family comes first." I imagined future struggles over this issue, bartering, begging with hand out for my share and that of his children. I recalled Sara's bitter complaints of Wole regularly sending, like a tithe, gifts to his mother and father—a radio to be used in a village without electricity, expensive lace to be worn once and then stored away. Gifts that honored them, that lavished respect on them for their years and their position as elders. Gifts that, in my eyes, said, "I love you first. I love you best."

"It's not fair to me." I stood up, outraged, my anger fueled by a sense that I had been cheated, denied.

"You knew my responsibilities long ago," he said.

"Have you no responsibility to me?"

"My family must come first. You know that."

How to face, fight the bulwark of this family that I thought would nestle me to its breast but instead was in competition with me for the man I loved. I felt myself sinking fast, anonymous and ignored. "I'm sorry, Femi," I said, fearing his reaction to my tirade. But he was steeling himself against me and answered my words with a frigid glance. When I touched him he merely turned out the light.

For the next week he did not speak to me. For the sin of questioning tradition I was cast outside the realm of his thoughts and consideration. Countless times he had done this, and each time I withered, unnourished by his attention. I received not even a glance. For Femi I simply ceased to exist. He ate dinner, looking stolidly at his food, and then retreated behind a newspaper for the rest of the evening. I sat before him, making conversation interspersed with pleas for a truce that went unheeded. He loomed, powerful and cruel, in the house, his silence a rack that stretched me, pulled until I nearly snapped. There was about him those moods, a confidence absent at other times, as if by bringing me pain he verified himself. Femi became a general, cold and indifferent, his boot marching across my face.

Finally I went to Jide and told him shamefacedly of our fight. Each time we argued Jide or some other family member restored my self-worth, talked to Femi, cajoled him out of his ill temper. I lay in bed and heard Jide talking to him in Yoruba about me; Jide, like all the others who interceded on my behalf, stressed my youth, my foreignness and my femaleness as things he must forgive and understand. In their arguments before Femi, they cited in my favor the family's acceptance of me, my attempts to assimilate some of the culture, concluding, "she has tried." And so, over breakfast the next morning Femi acknowledged me with a request for socks, a reminder to run an errand, the words slitting the silence like a razor. But never was I offered, "I am sorry" or "I love you," for he was as callous in peace as in war. And the need in me for his words, when I was denied them, became anger that I received nothing that nourished me as his wife, friend and lover. And I hated him for arbitrarily casting me into a twilight zone of despair. I hated him, and it took days to overcome the hate so that I could love him again.

During the summer break from school I traveled to Benin City with a colleague, Mr. Oyewale. Dr. Opubor called us in to work with the reporters of the paper whose board he chaired. We conducted a week-long series of journalism skills classes for reporters on *The Benin Observer*. Benin was a pleasant city of nearly unbearable contradictions. Unlike Lagos, which merely sprang up as a port city, Benin was planned. So the chaos that reigned in the capital city was largely absent. Its inhabitants, a mix of several different ethnic groups, lived peacefully together, blessed with humor and elegance of dress. Yet during our visit the city was in the throes of a crime wave so virulent that an 11 P.M. curfew had been imposed and was strictly enforced by gun-toting soldiers patrolling the city after dark.

A month later I traveled to Benin again for the weekend to sit on the *Observer*'s board of directors while it interviewed candidates for editorial and senior journalist positions. Dr. Opubor had asked me to join the board, along with the editor of the *Daily Times* for this occasion. So, at twenty-seven I sat at a conference table with a group of businessmen, chiefs and lawyers, determining the fate of individuals as eager for a job as I'd been in the past. I was heady with the first taste of a power I knew would have eluded me in the States. In Nigeria my skills and experience were held at a premium and had begun to open doors I had never even thought of approaching. I walked a trembling tightrope as I shaped ways to fulfill myself and make a contribution to a society that I regarded as home. In my work my status as an educated foreigner increased my ability to chisel out roles and occupations compatible with my ambitions. But in the tight, increasingly narrow world I lived in with Femi the culture that both straitjacketed and consoled me was beginning to emit sparks, as I increasingly struggled out of its hold.

During the summer break Tope returned to Nigeria without

Nike. At the welcoming party he told me that she had one more year of schooling to complete and then she would return. Within a few months he had set up a busy, lucrative medical practice in Ibadan.

At the end of the summer I was pregnant again. The child bloomed inside me, a flower opening its petals slowly, its leaves sustaining me. This was the child I wanted. The child I knew I could love. At the start of the pregnancy I felt stirring within me some self I had never known before. Heard the insistent cry of a woman I was about to become.

The first flakes of dead skin fell noiselessly to the ground, stacked beneath my feet. It would be months before the process was complete, and just like my child I struggled out of the womb.

My first child became, from inception, a conspirator against my dreams. My second child was an ally. I suffered only minor nausea for a few days in the first months, and only a light general fatigue. My breasts quickly swelled, becoming heavier, solid, the nipples darkening. When I undressed for bed Femi watched me, and his eyes poring over my body told me I was beautiful. When we made love, he suckled my new breasts, delighting in their bulk, rubbing them, like a hand, across his face. I treasured my body filled with child. Rubbing oil on my stomach to prevent stretch marks, I examined in fascination the dark line running from my navel to the pubic hair. By the fourth month my hair was thick and full, my skin luminous and clear. I began reading books on pregnancy and borrowed a book from Sara on the Lamaze method of painless childbirth.

My energy was nearly boundless, and in between teaching I began writing articles again. The government-owned broadcasting system purchased *Roots*, and the saga unfolded on Nigerian television. Nigerians were fascinated by what for most constituted a first encounter with the history of black America. For the *Daily Times* I wrote an essay examining the Nigerian reaction to the program. I sent my novel to the States for Sidney Offit to look at once more. He returned it with encouragement and some unexpected advice. "Put this aside for a while," he suggested, "and write about your life now, about Africa. That's a story that hasn't been told." I did put the novel aside, but more out of emotional fatigue and boredom with its themes and characters, which told me more about the manuscript than anything Sidney had said. But I flinched at the thought of examining my life as I had dredged the corners of memory and imagination for the novel. Instinctively I shunned his admonition to tell "a story that hasn't been told." I took my life for granted, standing drenched in all that it released. I guarded it too jealously to transform it into a narrative for others to dissect and judge. The magazine *Essence* commissioned me to write an article on "Blacks in Africa," and I was glad to be flexing journalistic skills that I had feared would turn flabby.

For the article I interviewed foreign wives, students and businessmen. Talking to them, the contradictions of my own experience began to gel. Their reactions to Nigeria, like my own, were ambiguous, maddening, exhilarating, baffling. Each one of them connected with some part of my own recent history. From anecdote and revelation we designed a wonderful, revealing collage. When I interviewed the men, no matter what their status (single or married) or occupation, no matter how long they had been in the country, much of their idealism remained intact. They spoke to me of power, of being unable to attain it in America but finding it in Nigeria. Because they were men, the society did not ask as much of them. Their options were greater and allowed them to improvise their destinies. But foreign wives were forced to bend to the collective will of clan, family and custom; or, if brave enough, to stake out an emotional territory of their own that acknowledged the conflicting claims of who they were and where they lived.

At the end of one interview a young black American man from Cleveland concluded, "But, you know, I put up with it all—the bad roads, the absence of light, no water in my pipes—and I bear it because I'm black in a black country. I tried to tell my friends at home how it feels to be a part of the majority, and it's so difficult to describe." At twenty-three he was a lecturer at the university, with plans to return to the States for a year and get more experience in his field of engineering, return to Nigeria, and start his own business. "I can get, for the first time in my life, beyond being black and just be me," he continued. "So I can turn that energy into growing and planning my future."

I closed my notebook and we sat sipping beers at the staff club. I thought, too, how used to the community of race I had become. How I relished the thought that on the trips to Benin the plane was flown by a black pilot. And how I was affirmed by the faces of the women that surrounded me—their hair, noses, their hips, broad like mine. Nigeria affirmed me and I wanted my child to be part of this. More than anything else, I wanted to give him a place in the black world and not just America.

For the article I interviewed Anita Okunwunmi as well. I had not seen her since she visited me in the hospital and was surprised by what I saw when we met again. The day I visited her she was working on a canvas. Dressed in blue jeans and a T-shirt, barefoot, she was possessed of a new steadiness. Unaccustomed to its fit, she still wore it somewhat uneasily. There were lines, too, around her eyes, and those mapping her forehead told me she was battleworn and that resignation had smoothed over her attempted rebellion. Gritting her teeth, standing fast, she had determined to sink her roots further into what appeared to be a quagmire. I wondered if even she knew why.

But when we sat down to talk, she quickly removed her mask.

In answer to one of my questions, she unleashed a bitter litany of complaints. "You can put this in the article if you want. The only reason I came to Africa was to be with my husband. And if I could've convinced him to stay in the States, believe me, I would've. They're hypocrites, all of them. Ranting on and on about African unity. Yet look at the tribalism. We spent a week in Abidjan last year, and every restaurant we went to they served the whites first. Look at the corruption. The ignorance. But I'm here now, and for better or worse, I guess, this is it." Summing up her five years in Nigeria, she issued a blanket condemnation. Despite my prodding and the adversary tone of some of my questions, she insisted on the validity of her bleak judgment.

Closing my notebook, I asked, "Why don't you go back to the States?"

"I didn't leave anything there, so I've nothing to go back to."

"How'd you and Banji meet?"

"I was on the rebound. I was engaged, then dumped quite unceremoniously when the bastard ran off with a friend of mine. Three weeks later I met Banji, and in six months we were married. I didn't love him. I was grateful to him for caring. So, to say thank you I gave him the only thing I had—myself. In the States kids weren't an issue. But here things changed overnight. His family disliked me immediately. He wanted me to bow to his parents, play meek and mild around the men. I wasn't used to that. Suddenly we argued all the time. Then, when I found out I couldn't have a child, everything fell to pieces."

"But you'll stay?" I asked.

"Sure, I'll stay. Because I don't have nightmares about his other wife anymore. Because I'm not strong enough to go back and build another life from scratch. What am I gonna go back for anyway? Who'd I go back to? My brothers? One's in jail, the other lives in Tucson with some white girl. I wouldn't know my father if he mugged me on the street, and my mother, my mother, she died a long time ago. I'm no college graduate. No beauty queen. How many men back home are gonna put three cars in front of the house and send me abroad every year? Sure, I'll stay. I've got no other choice."

20

Our son was born after a swift five-hour labor. My water broke at seven o'clock, just as Femi entered the house from work. It was not the flood I had expected, but rather a continuous trickle. Worry-free this time, I wanted to wait until contractions began before going to the hospital.

"Are you mad?" Femi asked in exasperation. "Don't you remember the last time?" Yetunde brought the overnight bag I'd had packed for a week and Femi hustled me into the car. At the hospital I was admitted, dressed in a gown, and Femi was told to leave. The woman in the bed next to me had been in labor seventeen hours. Her stomach was mountainous, and a stream of nurses and midwives continually hovered around her. She lay in a stupor broken periodically by animal-like groans of pain, yet when trounced by a contraction she writhed noiselessly, as though afraid to rumple the sheets.

At midnight my contractions began and I met each one with an intake of breath and the counting that allowed me to maneuver past the pain. Noticing my concentration, the nurse asked, "You are American?" When I shook my head yes, she smiled, saying, "All of you come here with your counting and this strange breathing. Does it help?" In the middle of a breath I nodded yes. The contractions were a wave, each one unique in intensity. The Lamaze diagrams and charts I'd religiously studied swirled in my head. The nature of the contractions, their length and fierceness, informed me where my baby was in my womb and how far it had traveled. When it settled into my vaginal canal, to get its head out I had to push with a strength I no longer had. There were no stirrups, so I had to lie on my side. Cursing the huge Ajayi head through clenched teeth, I pushed but could not get the baby's head out. I willed my body into a muscle—to no avail. Finally the nurse made an incision and instantly I felt the head bursting through. In seconds I heard a small outraged cry. I propped myself up on my elbows to see the child. Its eyes were tightly shut, its arms glued to its sides and its hands balled into fists. He was still in the fetal position, a mask of blood covering his face and body, as he yelped indignantly. I laughed heartily, amazed, relieved.

At noon Femi came into the ward, already aware he had a son. I had never seen him happier. In the bassinet beside my bed our son slept. Femi began to talk about the plans for the naming ceremony and all the things that had to be done to prepare for it. "Not now, Femi," I said. "Let's just enjoy the baby for a while."

That night I lay in bed, drinking in the sight of my child. The long-awaited deed had been done. I did not know then—could not know—that even higher hurdles loomed just ahead. Amazed by the miracle Femi and I had performed, I could not believe this child. Never had I written a line as beautiful as he, and I was sure I never would.

At home we were only allowed a few days alone, the child, Femi and I, before being besieged by relatives and friends. Femi traveled to Ado-Ekiti to bring his mother. Custom dictated that the grandmother (usually the wife's mother) come for three months to help with caring for the child. She arrived, and immediately her presence attracted relatives to the house as much to pay respects to her as to visit the baby. Genuinely respected, she was showered with gifts and attention. Two days before the naming ceremony the family decided on a name for the baby. Because of her position as an elder member, it was Femi's mother to whom we all deferred for a choice. Our child was named Akintunde (the spirit of the father returns) Babatope (praise be to God) Ajayi.

On the seventh day after our son's birth at eight o'clock in the morning, the "priest" arrived to conduct the ceremony that officially inducted our child into the community of his family. That night the house was filled with guests at the celebration party. From family and friends in the past week we had received customary gifts of money totaling almost a thousand dollars. I was in the bedroom with Tunde when Tope entered. Hugging me gently, he pressed a twenty-naira note into my palm. "For Tunde," he said, gazing at the baby happily, as though he was his own. Then he looked at me solemnly and asked, "Has Femi told you the history of our family?"

"No."

"Well, now that we have a new member I must tell the child. I must tell you. Come let us sit." He led me to the bed, where I rocked the baby on my lap. "The founder of our family, the first Ajayi, was an orisha priest for the oba of Benin. He served in the court of the oba for seven years, where he performed many miracles. So many that the oba rewarded him with gifts and titles. Then the tribal wars came. The enemy armies invaded Benin and those who survived were forced to flee. He wandered for many years and finally settled at Ado-Ekiti, where he met the first of his many wives." As I listened, before my eyes Tope became a *griot*, honoring through this retelling of legend, myth and fact his roots and their claim upon him. Their claim upon my son. Their claim upon me. The tale was long. The story twisted, turned, detoured through a centuries-old past. And soon the births, deaths, wars, marriages and migrations that spawned and shaped the Ajayis occupied the bedroom with us. Tope spoke from memory, rendering with an evangelist's zeal a past that stepped forward to anoint my son, as my father had once

brought forth the collective African-American past to anoint me.
The stories my father told placed me in a historical cosmos, a
universe of deed and belief. My father was a *griot*, too, honoring
ancestors connected by blood and faith to those who peopled
Tope's specific antiquity. At the end of his tale I gratefully
offered Tunde to him to hold, symbolically offering my son
to take his place in this lineage. Smiling at Tunde, he said,
"When he is older, Femi must tell the story to him again so he
will know who he is."

"I will see that he tells him," I promised.

"It is not enough to carry the name. You must know all that it
means," Tope said seriously. "Now you know who your husband
is and what your son will one day be."

The days of my maternity leave—shared with Yetunde, my
mother-in-law, and visits from Bisi—seemed unbearably long.
Some afternoons Femi's mother dressed herself in a gaily colored
buba and *iro* and strutted off to the nearby market where Bisi
had a stall. There she sat, happy and at ease in her milieu. On
other afternoons, after I had breast-fed Tunde, she held him in
her lap, rocking him to sleep. We talked in Yoruba—she telling
me anecdotes of her life with Femi's father, I going through my
photo album, telling her stories of relatives whose pictures lined
its pages. This was family and she sat rapt and attentive as I
pointed out cousins, nieces, uncles.

It was near the end of the dry season, a few weeks before the
rains arrived. Those weeks were always murderously hot, as if
raging that they would soon be overtaken by another season. In
the afternoon heat the ceiling fan whirled overhead. Femi's
mother sat fanning Tunde, her blouse removed, her chest covered by a beautiful white lace slip Jide sent her years ago from
Britain. Across her chest and back stretched a birdlike tattoo.
The bird's regal wings were spread for flight. Hundreds of tiny
marks embedded with blue dye formed the bird, giving to her
chest, with its breasts sagging like empty sacs to her waist, an elegant design that was disturbing and sensual. Bisi explained to
me that body designs were common on women of our mother-in-
law's age. Husbands found them sexually alluring. "You should
see my mother's," she said. "Ah, but the pain they endured. I've

seen it done and the blood is so much you would think they're killing a cow."

I quickly learned that motherhood was a high wire act sometimes performed without a net. During the first weeks Tunde cried for hours at night. Neither Femi nor I got enough sleep. During the day we were irritable and exhausted, eager to do battle over a word, a forgotten task, an innocent suggestion. Then, suddenly, there was no water coming through our pipes, and Femi was forced to bring plastic jugs of water home from his office. The absence of water sparked countless arguments, Femi charging that Yetunde used too much water to wash diapers, that I used too much for baths. Our child forced a thousand different adjustments in our relationship. Unaided, we lurched toward mastering this new role with a pain neither of us expected. Our child was the promise fulfilled. And because of our child, neither of us would ever be the same.

Soon I enlisted my mother-in-law's aid in these conflicts. Her influence with Femi was total, mine sporadic. One morning we sat in the living room after breakfast. Yetunde removed the dishes from the table. Femi sat on the sofa putting on his shoes, visibly gathering energy to face the work and the world teeming outside our door. As he moved to stand up, I looked at him and then at his mother. I entreated her to speak with Femi, telling her that his complaints about the water use were ridiculous with an infant now in the house. I asked her to tell him to have more patience and understanding of how hard things were for all of us. The words came in a rush—measured and heartfelt, each one honed over the past few weeks by frustration and fatigue. As I spoke, her face was passive, but her eyes, tiny and twinkling against the black landscape of her face, reflected understanding. She looked at Femi with a gaze that froze his movements. Instantly chastised by this look, he slumped back onto the sofa.

"But I am busy. I cannot bring water from my job twice a day."

Her long-fingered hand touched his arm to quiet him. In Yoruba she asked, "What would you do, have your wife bring that water herself? Your house is full now, blessed with a child.

You will not deny it water to drink, to be clean, for the mother to wash its clothes?"

"But what of Yetunde? She can fetch it."

"She is a small girl. How much water can she bring? The extra water is needed. You will bring it."

"So now you report me to my mother," Femi laughed, assessing me with surprise. The laugh conceded victory to me, confessed amazement at the bond I shared with his mother. "I will bring water in the afternoon and in the evening," he said, rising and kissing me lightly on the cheek as he headed for the door.

Without Femi's brothers, Tope and Jide, and without his mother I wondered how I would ever reach him. They were barriers and conduits between us. Their needs took precedence over mine, yet their voices translated my needs to him with a precision I despaired of ever learning. I—who wrote to save and manage my life, who sculpted from words explanations and truths, who confidently lectured to classrooms of students, who was awed by the potency and charm of words—was mute, as verbally incompetent as my child in the face of my husband's resistance. The passage of time had endowed me with few tools to shape a language to use with him. He was as dense as a rainforest, its trees twisted and tangled into an enticing threat, silent and fearsome. He was a country I had lived in, it seemed, all my life. He was a territory in which I found myself lost.

I sat in my study breast-feeding my son. Thick shafts of sunlight filtered through the curtains, creating geometric designs on the floor. The apartment was swathed in silence. My son and I were alone. The lean look of Tunde's birth, when his long, slender legs pushed his tiny feet from under the blanket, was soon abandoned for a chubbiness of which everyone approved. At five months he nursed greedily. The feeding ritual placed him as close to me as if he were still inside the womb. Joined soul to soul, his head was nestled against my breast, heavy with milk. His suckling noises and my awe at the elemental beauty of our communion locked us inside a time frame exclusive and consuming. Even then he did not allow others to ignore him. Merriment, whimsy and a confident awareness of his ability to charm and overcome indifference endowed him with a power that humbled both Femi and myself. I had always thought of babies as anonymous, ever wet, gurgling creatures whose only distinctions could be found in the genitals. But Tunde's cry was more virile and insistent than any I'd ever heard. In fact, I had simply never heard his cry before. It belonged distinctly to him. His staunch happiness and unflinching gaze earned us congratulations and surprised, envious comments on his nature. His gregarious temperament challenged my solitary tendencies. I had never imagined that a child could innately possess knowledge worthy of a parent's attention. But soon I was eager to learn.

At last we were a family, and for Femi the pressures to succeed financially gained momentum. Each evening after dinner he studied the soccer pool sheets and began to bet on them week after week without winning. Increasingly distracted and morose, minor problems became major insults to his ego, and I was accused of subverting his self-esteem. One weekend Yetunde went home to her village. While she was away I cooked the meals. I stood in the kitchen at the stove, Tunde strapped to my back in native fashion. From the living room I heard him explode, "How do you expect me to eat this?"

"What's wrong?"

"This. This rice is full of water."

"I'm sorry. Give me your plate. I'll cook it again," I said, reaching for the food.

"You deliberately disrespect me." He glared at me furiously. "I can't get a decent meal in my own house."

Tunde began to cry. I rocked him, trying to soothe him into silence. "Look, Femi, I'm sorry, okay?" I answered, bored and surprised by this drama. There was a vehemence in his voice that, were it softer, would have been a sob. The soggy rice symbolized every defeat of the past three years. "I said I'd cook it over."

"I won't eat anything prepared by your hand again," he declared, and stormed out of the house.

He was as good as his word, and by the next day he had stopped speaking to me as well. Yetunde returned and he ordered her to prepare separate meals for him. But for the first time in our five years together his silence failed to unnerve me. I watched in dismay and with cautious amusement his emotional gyrations. I surprised myself with my patience and, I could tell, Femi as well. More fatigued than hurt by his performance, I only wondered if I would have to watch such scenarios for the rest of my life. In the evenings he played with Tunde, loudly exaggerating his delight for my sake, then settled down to study his pool sheets or to look at television. After the first week I stopped greeting him when he entered the house because I received no answer. And I no longer inquired as to what he wanted to eat. I steeled myself for a long haul. The silence was broken after two weeks when he asked me to type up a report because his secretary had been out sick.

"You ask me to type a report for you, yet you haven't said good morning to me in two weeks," I shouted in amazement and anger. He stood before me in my study, a smirk crawling across his lips at this verification that I had been wounded by his stony attack. "No, I won't type it. Not until we talk. Talk about why we can't talk. Why we don't talk." He turned and went into the bedroom. I followed him, feeling rage welling up inside me. He lay on the bed thumbing through a magazine. "Our marriage is dying. I'm not just your wife now, Femi, I'm the mother of your child. I deserve better, more than this." Every hidden, ignored, rationalized injury bubbled to the surface. "What's wrong with us? We don't have a life together. We sleep and eat together. But that's not a life. We don't do things together, not even a drive on Sunday afternoons."

"I work hard during the week and want to rest on the weekends," he said.

"But what about me? Don't you think I might like to do something? Something with you? I don't feel connected to you anymore. I feel more distant than ever. And I'm not going to beg Jide to mediate for me this time. If you can talk to him, you can talk to me."

"What is it you want?" he asked impatiently, looking at me suddenly as if I had rudely interrupted him at work.

"To try to save what we have. Even our sex is no good anymore." He looked at me sharply. I thought of the joyless, passionless parody we acted out now in each other's arms. "You have to work at marriage."

"It's only you Americans who work at marriage," he sneered. "Africans don't have to." I stood up, wobbly and shaken, my confidence ambushed by the demons of doubt he had let loose.

The silence that I had seen as strength I then knew was merely rocklike rigidity. For a time I'd needed the stillness that filled the air of our union. The monotony, the silence that decorated our love assured me all was well. I looked at him now, turning to lie on his stomach as though he could not even bear to see my face, and knew there was no other man inside him I could release through my love. I'd run from even the echo of melodies before. Now I required the music of conversation and the healing powers of true intimacy. The petals had all dropped to the floor, for giving birth to my son had given birth to me.

21

It was 3 P.M. and the university staff club was virtually deserted. Walking up the steps, I spotted Ikpoi sitting at a table with another man. Even from a distance I could tell he was an American. Beads of sweat rose along my arms, my mouth was sandpaper dry with thirst. "God, just how hot is it?" I asked, sitting down next to him.

"Who knows?" he shrugged, taking a sip from a glass of beer. "The weather in Africa is a chronic condition, not a variable."

"Maybe that's why I haven't heard a weather report in three years," I said. "The heat defies explanation."

"Lagos defies everything," the other man said, extinguishing the fat stub of a cigar in an ashtray.

Ikpoi introduced us. "Marita Ajayi, Lee Houston."

He rose slightly in his chair and reached to shake my hand. Small tufts of gray hair sprouted at his hairline and poked out from behind his ears. His eyes lived beneath an unruly forest of eyebrows. Light brown marbles rolling across the floor of my face, the eyes informed me they had seen nearly everything. The blue and white dashiki fell over his shoulders and arms as though it had never lain anywhere else.

Ikpoi told him, "Marita is a lecturer in our department." He had been the African correspondent for an American newspaper for the past year. "How's Dorothy?" Ikpoi asked.

"She left for New York yesterday. She wants to go through with the divorce."

"Do you?"

"No, but I won't contest it."

To distance myself from the secrets they were sharing, I went to the bar and ordered a Coke. Waiting for the order, I saw them huddled at the table, Ikpoi using his hands to accentuate what he was saying, Lee absently dawdling with his index finger through the cigar ashes. When I returned, they sat savoring some small victory both had managed to win, one that they shared with magnanimity. "So where are you from?" he asked. We talked amiably, with casual meaninglessness, disrobing skeletal outlines of our pasts. At four o'clock Ikpoi left to pick up his children from school. I expected Houston to leave with him, but he didn't.

It had been weeks since I had been required to converse. My feelings and desires no longer existed for Femi. Our silence had declared war. Neither side was winning. For protection I had turned inward, constructed a cerebral existence built with the raw material of wishes and prayers. I no longer counted the days since his voice last addressed me. I no longer cared. So this conversation pulsed with half thoughts, pauses and a hesitancy from me that I had never experienced before.

"How do you like living here?" he asked.

"It's hard . . . sometimes," I said quietly. "And sometimes it's the easiest thing I've ever done."

"Do you know many other Americans?"

"A few." I sat up straight in the chair, suddenly aware of my slouch. "What I mean is—"

"Should I fill in the blanks?" he asked. I looked at him quizzically. "The open spaces. The holes in your conversation. You seem to have a lot on your mind."

"I'm sorry," I apologized, looking at him and marshaling my attention.

He called for the waiter and paid for his drink. "I'd better start back to the mainland," he said, rising.

Responding too fast, like a child bargaining for a return of attention or love, I said, "I'd like to talk to you sometime. I really would. About your work. What's happening in the States. What's happening here."

"I'd like that too," he said with a trace of a smile that comforted me more than I could bear.

A week later I entered my office and found him sitting on my desk. In his battered but sturdy Peugeot we drove to a nearby Chinese restaurant for lunch. He was brimming with anecdotes about African heads of state and various government officials, having just returned from covering the civil war in a North African nation. Soon I learned that he was a lawyer for ten years before switching to journalism. That he played the flute, was knocked out, like me, by Ngugi Wa Thiong'O's *Petals of Blood* and owned a farm in Sierra Leone. Our conversation bubbled, aromatic and strong. Over coffee I was charged. The sound of my voice no longer hit my ears like static shock.

Afterward he suggested we drive to Bar Beach. "I really shouldn't," I said. I hesitated, standing before his car.

"Why?"

"I've got a nine-month-old son and—"

"You've a house girl, right?"

"Yes."

"She's good with him?"

"Yes."

"Get in," he ordered with a wave of his hand. At Bar Beach we removed our shoes and dug our toes into the sand. Because it was a weekday, we were the only ones there for relaxation. We shared the beach with a small group of Ghanaians who built huts along the shoreline. They were flooding Nigeria to escape Ghana's economic woes. Beggars and hustlers passed by, offering cheap trinkets and African cloth.

"Now tell me about you."

"There's not much," I said, making circles with my index finger in the sand. "I'm a wife. Somebody's mama. I teach and write."

"That's a lot to be proud of."

"Mostly I feel like a ghost these days. Like I'm sleepwalking through my life. Something's happening to me independent of my control. I feel helpless witnessing it, and yet I somehow feel reassured."

"Postpartum depression?"

"I wish it were only that. Have you children?" I asked him.

"Yes, they're in college. Harvard and Brown."

"Nice, respectable schools," I mused sarcastically. "Your bootstraps must have been quite strong." I looked at him and he leaned forward to kiss me. I stood up, dusting the sand off of my dress.

"What's wrong?"

"I didn't expect that. I don't know if I want it."

We drove back to the university in silence to get my car. When I reached to open the car door he held me in. "I'd like to see you again."

"I don't know," I said, squirming with the knowledge of how badly I wanted to see him again.

"If you don't mind," he teased.

"I don't know. Midterms are next week and—I just don't know. Call me at school."

"You know the phones don't work." He paused and then asked in exasperation, "Is this really necessary?"

"Yes. For me it is. I'm falling out of love with my husband. I'm a bad risk right now."

"I still love my wife. So we're even."

I leaned back against the seat. "I haven't talked with a man like we talked today in years. I haven't needed to. Now I do. I'm afraid of that need. You should be too."

"I've been under fire before. Your need isn't lethal. It's not a bullet."

"Next week?" I asked, getting out of the car.

"Tuesday at 12:30," he said. "If I have to go out of town, I'll get a message to you."

Soon we were having lunch once a week. And soon I realized that I wanted him. I wanted him because he still loved his wife and would not require that I shape the shadow I cast to fit inside his. I did not want love but affirmation. He went to Cairo for ten days and when he returned we had lunch at his house. Impressive African sculptures were perched on mahogany tables and were stationed in corners. When he saw me assessing the decor in obvious awe, he said, "Oh, don't feel intimidated. All this stuff is rented." Then he laughed loudly, hugging me like a brother and friend. We ate at a long, gleaming mahogany table, facing each other at opposite ends. The steward padded around us silently, the silverware and plates scratching the table's surface, the only sound filling the room. We had run out of words. When the steward cleared the dishes, Lee came toward me like a lion who had cornered his prey. Up to now we had been remarkably chaste. Finally we kissed. His was a taste I meant to get used to. In his bedroom, beneath his hands my clothes melted onto the floor. Eager, flushed from weeks of anticipation, we scrambled into bed, where he became a magic wand, bringing forth from me a low, ecstatic moan from the most parched, barren acres of my mind. A moan from the patch of earth my despair had convinced me would never be fertile again. I shivered with ripples of pleasure, amazed at this rekindling of desire. We had talked with words. Now our bodies chattered, wondered aloud, in an improvised language that was a secret code and common knowledge.

At home silence still reigned. Recklessly seeking to force a reaction from Femi, I dressed up every day, not only on the days I would see Lee. Forsaking the bland, drab colors and styles that I hid beneath before, I bought colorful clothes, retrieved dresses from my suitcase I had not worn since my days in New York. Dresses that were not uniforms but poems celebrating who I was and who I could be. I became vain, self-conscious, spending time before the mirror in the morning. I strutted through the apartment, provocative and confident, teasing Femi, daring him to lay claim to me and to the love that was fast withering inside me. And because he could not speak, his eyes watched me with a muted concentration. He feigned disinterest, yet behind his glance, which tried hard to avoid my eyes, I felt him looking at me in a way he never had before. My insurrection frightened him and in his silence he planned a strategy for his survival, though not necessarily mine.

I came home from the hospital with Tunde one afternoon to find the front door locked from the inside, the bolt lock pulled across the front. There was no sign of Yetunde, so I went to Jide's house and found Yetunde there. She told me that in the afternoon Femi returned home and told her to come to Jide's. She saw him lock the door. When Jide returned from work, I told him what happened. That evening he accompanied me to the house. When we entered the house, Yetunde took Tunde and put him to bed.

"This warfare between you must end," Jide pronounced solemnly. He turned to Femi and spoke to him in Yoruba, chastising him for his action.

Femi exploded. "It's her! Why don't you ask her who she's been seeing. Ask her to tell you how she's changed." For the first time in two months his face was unfrozen. And as he hurled the charges at me, I saw his face tinged with hurt—and also with relief that he could finally release these feelings. His charges begged for my attention, asked me to look at him again, as I had refused to do, afraid to meet his glance.

"And you can say these things to Jide but not to me," I charged.

Jide turned to me and asked, "Are these things true?"

"We can't talk, he won't talk. That's the problem." I sat before them both, struggling to explain. "I need to feel loved. Like I matter. Not like a footnote to his life. I've been neglected, ignored."

"Brother," Femi interrupted, "you know my business, how badly it's been going."

"You hadn't a penny when I met you!" I screamed. "I picked up my life and followed you here then. Do you think it was only because you thought you'd be rich one day? The money doesn't matter to me."

"But it matters to me," he shouted.

"While you worry about money, you let me waste away. You want to talk about money. I want to talk about what's really important—us." Jide stood up and told us both to be quiet. Jide told Femi in Yoruba that he must try harder with me, spend more time with me. He urged me to have patience with Femi, to understand his frustration. I looked at Femi's face and it was hopeful, looking unflinchingly at me for the first time in weeks. It was a face offering love but not understanding. As Sara said, he could forgive me for the lover he suspected I had, but not the emotional self-sufficiency I brandished like a sword. I turned from his face because I knew I didn't have the patience Jide told me I must have. I was afraid of dying. I feared Femi's indifference would kill the new me bursting forth. The me I couldn't help. We both answered Jide with silence and assessed each other wordlessly. Jide told us he would return later in the week and that he expected to see us reunited. When he left, I went into the bedroom to check on Tunde.

As I came out, Femi stood in the doorway. He placed his hands on my shoulders and kissed my forehead gentler than I'd ever felt. "Will you go back to the way you were before?" The plea was quiet yet desperate.

"Femi, I can't. I don't know that woman anymore. I couldn't find her if I tried." As I leaned on his chest for support, he tensed and warned me, "You'll have to if you want to live in this house."

So, stalemated, we both temporarily retreated, enemies determined not to give an inch, shocked by the stubbornness of the foe. A veneer of normalcy covered our actions. Yet the denial, the retreat, was always there. When Femi touched me, desire froze. I forced myself to respond, but my performance was inadequate and he turned away in disgust midway through the exercise. I no longer knew if I loved him. I no longer cared whether I did or not.

Several months earlier the editor of *Essence* had assigned me to write a story on Nigerian–Afro-American marriages. The letter she wrote me outlining the story revealed her excitement about such a story and her feeling that I was the ideal person to write

it. She wanted an account, she said, that would be honest yet
balanced and fair. Riddled even then with premonitions of the
conflicts that later consumed me, I procrastinated and put off for
nearly two months beginning the interviews that would form the
basis of the story. I did not know it then, but I was terrified of
looking at other marriages, fearing what other unions might reveal about my own. I feared that the rationalizations and illusions that were beginning to unravel and that had given
my love for Femi so much of its tenacity would disintegrate
under the searchlight of questioning and challenge. I knew I
could not dig into the lives of others and leave my own life and
assumptions undisturbed. So, even as I laid the letter on my desk
the day I received it, my heart rumbled as though overthrown,
just as the realities that story revealed unalterably changed so
much between Femi and me.

As the tensions between Femi and me increased, and unable
to bear life in my own home, I invaded the homes of others and
found reflections of the same tensions that were splintering my
own life. I spoke to black American women and Nigerian men,
and in over a dozen conversations was overwhelmed by their
candor and willingness to admit to the ambiguities that charac-
terized their special unions. With startling honesty they all bore
witness to the endurance of love and the failure of understanding. Their secrets burdened me to the point of emotional
exhaustion, but in the end they endowed me with a knowledge
of myself and of Femi for which I was grateful.

When I completed the story, I asked Femi to read it. I handed
the twenty-five-page manuscript to him as seriously as though I
were handing him my life. After glancing at the first three pages
indifferently, he tossed it on the coffee table, where it lay for the
next two days, untouched, until I put it in an envelope bearing a
New York City address. By the time the article was published I
would be in the States, and I'd have written a new ending to the
article just as I'd had to revise the close of this chapter of my
life.

When I told Sara about Lee and the break between me and
Femi, she gazed at me with a new, strange kind of respect. Her

look took me into her confidence the way none of her words had before. "Do you love him?" she asked me about Lee.

"I'm beginning to by default. It's the only way I have of saying I'm still alive."

"Love by default," she laughed. "How does it feel?"

"As awful as it sounds."

"Why do you feel you have to make a choice?" I realized she was talking about Lee and Femi. I had been talking about my life. "I've always thought you were too serious, Marita. Too intense. It's only an affair," she said.

"But what happens to me? Whether I love one of them or both of them? What about me?"

"If you make peace with the husband, the marriage you have, you'll survive—and quite well. No worse than the rest of us. If you can't, I don't know."

My affair with Lee took place on the run. Ever in transit, he almost always had just returned or was preparing to leave to investigate a famine, a war, a coup. From Kenya he brought me an ivory bracelet, from Senegal a framed batik wall hanging given to him by one of that country's best known artists. Though our time together slipped by all too fast through the sieve of my expectations, he was an anchor stationing me temporarily to happiness. Having no time for revelation, he offered crumbs of his inner self. I, however, presented him with a whole loaf. Slicing it thin, he digested it at his leisure.

Sipping wine from Zimbabwe in glasses imported from England, we lay on sheets his wife had bought in New York. My probing had touched a nerve as I asked him about his children. Finishing the wine, he placed the glass on the night stand. Helplessly I watched a mask form over his face as he slid beside me, his head beneath my breast, his hands rubbing my back.

"Why do you ask?" The tone of his voice attempted to negotiate a way out of answering.

"I'm curious. Now that I have a child, I wonder what it's like to watch them grow. How do they change? How do they change you?"

"You'd get a better answer from my wife," he said, his breath tickling my skin.

"Why?"

"I wasn't around much to watch them grow. I was too busy putting food on the table and a second car in the garage." I sat up on one elbow and let my fingers roam through his jungle growth of hair. "My old man was a pullman porter. Most of his life he spent riding trains up and down the East Coast waiting on white folks. I grew up with only the vaguest notion of what fathers were supposed to do. So when I had kids of my own, I had to improvise. I found out pretty soon that I'm better at the flute. Why all the questions?"

"I'm a journalist, too, remember."

"Remind me never to have another affair with a writer," he jested, pulling me on top of him. I lay my head on his shoulder and wondered if he had sensed my discontent. I had yet to divulge the level of my misery, fearing that to do so would violate the etiquette of our frivolous, painfully intense attachment. Yet depression grew like cancerous cells within me, and I knew the secret would spill out on its own one day, hot lava scarring us both.

The day Femi beat me I was almost relieved, for it decided everything. I no longer remembered whether the tone of my voice or a casual look of insolence sparked his fury, but in a split second he grabbed me, whirling me away from the stove. Pushing me against the back door, his hands turned into claws digging into my neck. Retreating into stoic silence and horrified disbelief, I let my body go limp. Again and again he slammed me against the door, yet even as he slapped me, he held back the full force of his strength, for this beating was meant to warn rather than hurt me. Tunde crawled on the floor at my feet, oblivious to our storm, playing with a ball. Yet my refusal to cry, scream or fight back fueled Femi's anger and suddenly he stopped. Trembling, I slid in a heap onto the floor. Reaching for Tunde, I held him tightly as he tried to squirm out of my grasp. Femi reappeared, his belt dangling from his hand. The sight of the belt nearly stopped my heart. Standing wide-legged, blocking the doorway, he whipped the belt across his palm three times.

"Now say one word. Say one word and I'll beat you, I swear."

The look on his face dug my grave and buried me. Tunde squirmed in my arms, rebelling against the tightness of my hold. "You can leave if you want," he shouted, his anger making his breath come heavy and rasping. "But you can't take that child. If you try to, I'll find you no matter where you go." The sound of the belt, lashlike in the air, and his look pinned me to the floor. His rage spent, he slipped the belt through his pants loops, buckled it and left the house.

Hustling Tunde into his car seat, I drove to Sara's but found no one home. From there I went to Anita's. With Tunde on my back, native style, I paced her living room, telling her about the fight and then about Lee. "And today is the first time he's ever threatened me about the baby."

"I'd take him at his word on that if I were you."

"I won't take another beating. Never," I insisted angrily. "I've got to leave, but I don't know how."

"Let me show you something," she said. I followed her into her bedroom, where she got a key out of a drawer. From the bedroom we walked to a small room that I assumed was a boy's quarters. She opened the door with the key. The room was filled with a dozen trunks, suitcases and boxes of varying sizes and shapes. On the boxes were labels with the names of American girls in the States.

"But what is all this?" I asked.

"Stuff left behind by girls who left. They'd come and ask me to keep a box or suitcase until they could send for it. Some I've never heard from again."

"How did they leave?"

"A couple got divorced. The others just left. Some left with their husbands' knowledge. Quite a few escaped."

"Escaped?"

"Escaped," she said.

I looked at the suitcases again and for the first time that day I felt near tears. "Does it always end like this?"

"Not always. But more often than any of us like to think about." In the living room I removed Tunde from my back and lay him on the sofa. At the bar Anita mixed me a drink. "You want to hear the stories those boxes can't tell?" she asked, hand-ing me the drink.

"Not particularly."

"I've loaned money to girls to buy tickets to get back home. Chartered taxis to take girls and their kids to Kano to get a flight to the States 'cause it's safer to leave from there than Lagos."

"Is this your revenge?" I asked.

"In a way it is," she said quietly. "They all shake their heads and pity me. But it's Anita. Childless, foolish Anita they come to when they have to leave and can't find a way. They forget about Banji's other wife then. They forget about feeling superior. But I help them 'cause, Lord knows, one day I might need somebody to buy a ticket to Kano for me. So what do *you* want to do?"

"What I'd like to do is get a divorce and stay here. This place is my life. It's taken me three years to get where I am now."

"Do you want your son?"

"Of course."

"Then I'd advise you to leave. You can get a divorce. But there's no guarantee you'll get your child, especially if this busi-ness about your affair comes out."

"I've seen the effects of Femi's anger on his family. It's awful and I've always dreaded the day it would be turned on me. But, unlike his family, I have no one to plead my case with him. No one in his family will help me negotiate with him for both my freedom and my son. He'll simply never let me have Tunde. I know it. Tunde is all he has. But now he's all I've got too. What will I do?"

"Can you tom?"

"Tom? What do you mean?"

"I mean, can you make love to Femi, smile at him, cook good meals for him? Can you tom long enough to work on a way to get out of here?"

"Anita, I don't know. After today—"

"You've got no other choice, Marita. If you want your child, you'd better learn to love Femi like you used to while we figure out how you can get away."

22

Femi sat across from me eating with relish the food I had prepared. When Yetunde set the platter of plantains—crisp, golden, their sweet fragrance scenting the air—the bowl of rice—fluffy white and steaming—and the chicken stew on the table, his eyes brightened with approval. The patiently cooked food, evidence of my labor, instilled in him a singular joy. Nothing else I said or did, save giving him a son, ever earned me similar commendation. Idly I picked at several spoonfuls of rice and three plantain slices on a saucer. Anxious and overwrought, I had virtually stopped eating. Dragging me into her bedroom one afternoon, Anita stood me before the mirror and with a shake of her head declared, "You look awful. What's the matter with you?" Only then did I notice the lifeless pallor of my skin and the dullness of my eyes. She brought a scale from the bathroom which revealed that I had lost ten pounds in two weeks. Femi said nothing of my lack of appetite or my appearance, so grateful, I imagined, was he for the return of a surface calm to our lives. As Anita advised, I had begun to successfully feign passion and had squashed the fires of insurgency that once lit up my face. But at night in my study I wrote letters to Wanda, to relatives and friends. In the letters I had conversations I knew I would never have with Femi about growth and change. I typed the letters until my fingers ached, but they were life rafts that kept me from sinking.

To my best friend I wrote:

December 8, 1978

Dear Wanda:

Congratulations on the rave reviews of the play. Look out Broadway! I am so proud of you. Wish I'd been there for the opening night. Congratulations, too, on Charles. He sounds like just what you've wanted and needed. It's so strange, the cycles our lives have taken. When you are in love, I'm alone, and when I'm as happy as I imagine I'll ever be, gloom has camped out on your doorstep. I guess we're destined never to experience the same things simultaneously. I could almost see how happy you are by reading the letter. I hope it lasts forever.

I found your reaction to the crisis between Femi and me characteristically cautious and supportive. Your assertion that what I feel is postpartum depression may have some validity, but my doubts about how viable my love for Femi is and how useful it will be in the future runs too deep, strikes, whenever I think of it, too many nerves that send me howling in emotional pain. I wish I could chalk it all up to depression, but I can't. My friend Sara seems threatened by the instability of my marriage and my determination to ask questions no matter what the answer, and has gradually withdrawn the support I'd come to depend on. Another American girl, Anita Okunwunmi, who's helping me through a lot of this day by day, asked me the other morning what Femi and I had in common. To my amazement, I sat before

her fumbling for an answer. Even as my mind raged with silence, I was confident that I would be able to rattle off a list
of interests and desires we shared. After three minutes I
gave up. For the first time I've really been thinking about
my relationship with Femi, looking at it, turning it upside
down. What I've discovered is a host of incompatibilities
that have always been there but that, because of my need, I
had denied or ignored. I can't lie any longer. The things that
I value—intimacy, sharing, communication—do not exist as
priorities for Femi. They never have. But in times when he
was more optimistic about his future they did not stand out
in such bold relief. The thought of living with someone so
totally out of touch with his and my emotions is a sacrifice
I'm not prepared to make. How does one live with a stone
wall? Scale it? Blow it up? Wither in its shadow? I choose
to walk away from it.

You took the news of my affair as casually as I seem to
have slipped into it. I wish it were, as you suggest, just a
simple matter of relaxing, flowing with it and being careful.
How starved I am, not so much for sex as for affection and
attention, for someone to listen to me and, just as important,
to whom I can listen. Yet my affair with Lee, as exhilarating
as it is, has enhanced my unhappiness with Femi. And this
affair cannot, will not, save my marriage. I can't bear the
thought of Femi touching me now. I am so ridden with guilt
and memories of what I share with Lee.

I feel as though I am walking through a kind of death that
lifts only intermittently, when I look at my son or lie in my
lover's arms. Tunde is fine, firmly entrenched in the oral
stage. Everything, and I mean everything, goes into his
mouth. His cheerfulness seems limitless. I only wish it was
contagious.

love,
Marita

January 15, 1979

Dear Wanda:

The poems you sent me were quite good, I thought, as first efforts anyway. You'll find, of course, that the longer you "live" with the work the more you can give to it, and if it's workable as an idea, the more it simply takes on a life of its own. Hey, kid, will our friendship survive the competition? Hope you received the batiks I sent, in time for your birthday.

You asked if I still love Femi. In a manner I do, because of six years together and because of a child. But that is all. He has asked me to go back to being the woman I was before. That is his ground rule for us staying together. He might as well ask me to go back to being twelve. I can't do either. Friends tell me to wait until his business takes off. Then, they assure me, things will improve. But will financial success make him more sensitive? Or will it make him merely more driven to maintain that success and cap it with even more, perhaps showering me with material benefits but erasing me from the internal landscape of his life?

I'm leaving. I must. There is no other way. God knows, it won't be as easy as typing it on this page. There will be guilt, sorrow, regret. But I've got all that staying here.

love,
Marita

To my mentor, Sidney Offit, I wrote:

January 12, 1979

Dear Sidney:

I have just finished reading Judith Rossner's Attachments *and rereading* Madame Bovary, *two books that pretty accurately reflect my present frame of mind. Reading Rossner's powerful weaving of mutual dependencies and her dissection of human frailty was like drinking one of those mixed drinks that look harmless, so you down a couple of them, but an hour later you can't stand up to get your coat. She's not just a damn good writer, she's sneaky too. Using the "two women marry Siamese twins" angle to get you into the book, whetting our voyeuristic appetites (my God, how do they do it!!!!!), then painting a portrait of love, friendship, marriage and all those universals so skilfully we pretty soon leave behind the desire to be titillated. I read Madame Bovary for the first time when I was sixteen and appreciated it as just a wonderful love story. Now, at twenty-nine, I know better. I still don't know how Flaubert did it. Do you?*

My own life of late has begun to resemble the lives of Rossner's two heroines and Emma Bovary as well. I'm starring in my own soap opera as what has been my life up to now unravels at the seams.

I don't think I make a very good heroine. I detest center stage, prefer the role of omniscient narrator to main character. But it's happening and it feels like one of those episodic novels by Fielding or Thackeray with 156 chapters and titles like "In Which Marita Makes Plans for a Great Escape." Yes, and it has all the required elements—love lost, adultery, a war over child custody, emotional and physical abuse. But since this is my life and not a novel, I can't scratch out whole sections that seem absurd, change dialogue or even write the happy ending I dream of so desperately every night.

You've been urging me to write about my life and experiences here, and, as you know, I've resisted your suggestion. But now that this life is falling apart I suddenly see the dramatic potential, the pulse, blood and guts of it all. Stepping outside my life I see that it would make a good story. Diagnosing my life in this manner positively gives me the chills. And I feel like a vulture circling over the ruins of all I hold dear, sucking its bones till they are white. Does this mean I had to lose love, marriage, Africa in order to write about it? What a price to pay. As an artist, will the price always be this high?

It looks like I'll be coming back to the States in a few months. I've enclosed a copy of my résumé. I'd appreciate your looking at it and offering any job advice you can.

I'm not Emma Bovary. Flaubert did it. But in the end I can't buy it, even as I weep. I decided back in 1968 to re-

ject forever madness, suicide, permanent depression. That's when I determined what kind of woman I was going to be. I'm either too stubborn or too stupid to follow Emma Bovary's path. Surviving and believing in tomorrow is just a habit I can't break.

Yours,
Marita

But that evening, as he ate, now and then throwing a casual glance toward the television screen, Femi's face was utterly content. My face looked at his with just a trace of a smile, open, devoid of subterfuge or secrets. Rarely now did I allow my look to relax into mere neutrality for fear he would interpret that as a testing ground for future hostility. Finished, he pushed his plate away and stretched, yawning loudly. I had learned as well to maintain a steady stream of conversation, for if silence overtook us it might burst like a mushroom cloud into the words, bitter and accusing, that still hid in all the corners of our house. "Bisi brought the *agbada* and *sokoto* for Tunde today," I said.

"Let me see it."

Tunde's first birthday was two weeks away, and with Bisi's help we were planning a birthday party. The traditional garb for such an occasion was native dress consisting of matching material for parents and child. Bisi had sewn a dashiki and robe and pants for Tunde to wear. In the bedroom I dressed in a blouse and wrapper made of the same material and wound the matching *galae* around my head. When I gave Femi Tunde's suit, he surveyed it proudly. It was a miniature of his own and even included a *fila*, or tiny cap. Femi laughed, sliding into Pidgin English at the thought of his son dressed like a man, saying, "Tunde go be big man o." Folding the outfit, he placed it beside him on the sofa and appraised me. "Come here," he asked, reaching for me. I sat beside him, and as if for the very first time he placed my head on his shoulder. His hands fondled and caressed me, hugged me tight, as though he suspected my intended flight and hoped by brute strength alone to make me stay. He kissed me and I surrendered. But the kiss reminded me that when I had gone he would never understand or admit the reason for my leaving. I opened my eyes and scanned his face—handsome, entirely stripped of cruelty. The face I had once loved more than my own. How would I leave it? "We are happy now," he said, his lips planted on my neck. "Don't you see? We are happy," he insisted.

My arms held him tighter and I whispered in his ear, "Yes, Femi, we are as happy as we will ever be."

After eleven months underfoot, Tunde finally learned to stand. Crawling around the apartment, he claimed it as his personal dominion. His hands splashed inside the plastic water containers, he imprisoned himself between the legs of the dining room chairs, foraged through the bottom shelves of my bookcases, adopting early on a hearty appetite for the printed word. In the pantry he inspected beans, overturned bags of rice. Resisting our attempts to teach him to stand up, he studiously fell onto his bottom within seconds of being placed in a standing position. Then one evening while we sat reading the papers, he embarked upon his own independent struggle to stand. Like an ant tackling a hill of sand he gripped the legs of the coffee table. His chubby palms repeatedly lost their grip. His face became suddenly determined, impatient on the fifth try, and it was this will that propelled him into a standing position. Holding onto the table, he progressed to the side where Femi and I sat. I had watched his progress, biting my lip, silently rooting for him, wiping away a tear when he stood, wobbly but determined not to fall. I touched Femi's arm. He dropped the paper. When I pointed to his son, he looked down at his side where Tunde stood, his arms reaching out to us both.

In those final weeks I alternately clung to and repudiated my affair with Lee. When we were together, I sniped at the tranquillity he offered, bludgeoned the affection I felt for him with sarcasm and self-flagellation. The more patience he exuded, the more fury I turned on him. My anger at having to bury a career, a life, friendships and a future consumed me. And when I divulged my secret, it was in a manner as melancholy as it was oblique.

The waves lapped hungrily at the shoreline of Bar Beach that day, encroaching with monotonous, virile intensity. Frothy mountains of foam capped the waves, muscular arms lifting the ocean's skirt. A German family, parents and a toddler with a Dutch boy haircut, stood a few feet away from the approaching tide. The child, held in his father's arms, squealed in delight each time a wave landed against the shore. His squeals echoed in the afternoon air around the squalling of sea gulls gliding overhead. Lee sat in a deck chair watching me as I looked at the ocean. His stare—puzzled, hostile—pinned me to an imaginary wall. The same wall I'd built, brick by brick, between us.

"I want you to drive me across the border next week, can you do it?" I asked, addressing the ocean more directly than him.

"What for?"

"I'm leaving my husband. I'm going home and I can't risk leaving from Lagos; someone I know might see me." I turned from the ocean to look at him and saw that his face had crumpled into jagged lines of disbelief. As he opened his mouth to speak, I turned on my stomach, lay my hands flat on the sand, and told him why. My voice cracked with fatigue as I told him the story—less than I told Anita but more than I revealed to Dr. Opubor the day before, when I had asked for a leave of absence because of "personal problems." Telling him reminded me how desperately tired I was of being unhappy, consumed with anger and therefore able to know nothing else. And as I told him and watched his face soften, I felt that the day this present would be past was light-years away.

"Why did you wait so long to tell me?"

"I didn't know what you'd say. What you'd think. The sooner I told you, the sooner I'd have to deal with saying good-bye."

"And there's no way you can stay?"

"I'm afraid of losing my son. To try to stay would give my husband the opportunity to make my life a greater hell than it already is."

"Are you sure you're doing the right thing?"

"I'm not doing the right thing!" I shouted. "I'm doing the only thing I can do. I'm no good at lies, Lee. Can't tell them and I'm worse at living them."

He eased next to me in the sand. "But what about your idealism? You always said you were happy here."

"I am. Africa, Nigeria is not the problem. My marriage is."

"Let me be supremely selfish, let me be a real pig for a moment and ask you to stay for me."

"Lee, I can't. I just can't risk it."

"I could get you another place to stay. I've got contacts, I know some honest lawyers."

"Can you promise me my son? Swear that even if I get custody of him in a country where the children belong, by tradition and law, to the father, that my husband won't take him anyway? I've lived with the man. I've loved him. I know his anger, can smell it like a thunderstorm invading the sky. Anger is the only weapon he has left now, and I won't lose my life or my son to it."

Resignedly he asked, "Have you got your ticket?"

"Yes."

"Do you need any money?"

"Yes."

"I'll give some to you in dollars the day we leave. If I can't take you, I'll arrange for someone who can."

"Thank you, Lee, I—"

"Don't say thank you. This is something I really wish I didn't have to do."

"So do I, baby, so do I."

III. Coming Home

23

It was mid March but winter clung steadfastly to the East Coast. The snow flurries swirling, furious and windblown, along Washington's streets matched my own sense of disorientation. The atmosphere outside was as hard and frozen as my emotions. Only moments after I'd locked the car door and settled Tunde in my lap, my uncle, who was driving me to his house from National Airport, asked, "What happened?"

Responding to the command in his voice, I sputtered out, "It wasn't working anymore—"

"What do you mean it wasn't working?"

"I was miserable. I changed and he didn't."

He leaned forward, turned down the volume of the country and western music station, and said with such urgency that an answer became obligatory, "But you still haven't told me what really happened."

Fatigue clenched every muscle in my body as the To-go/Paris/New York/Washington flight fast-forwarded in my memory. Three hundred dollars in overweight in Togo, even after packing only necessities. A four-hour layover at Charles de Gaulle Airport outside Paris, pacing its opulent glass-and-chrome interior while a blizzard raged outside. The final New York to D.C. flight after a call to Wanda. Suffering from jet lag and exhausted, I turned to my uncle. "I guess I can't tell you what happened because I still don't know myself."

After a week in Washington, buying winter clothes and extending a lifeline to friends and relatives via phone calls and letters, I knew I had to leave. Washington was claustrophobic. I feared suffocating through sheer inertia. D.C. had launched me into the world. Now, greedily, it was the world I called home. Washington was too small. I simply knew it too well. I wanted to see Wanda, touch base with New York, even though I knew I could not live there again, for it was where I'd met Femi. I was withdrawn and anxious, tense as a fugitive. Cringing at the thought yet expecting it, I waited for the fallout, wondered in waking and nighttime dreams what Femi did the day he came home to find us gone, with a good-bye note on the dinner table. I wondered what he would do to strike back at or reclaim us.

Wanda was as composed as I was fractured. Though I initially resented her serenity in the face of my despair, I later came to depend on it. She had moved to a larger apartment on Manhattan's West Side. After helping me bring my luggage and Tunde upstairs from the taxi, she hugged me. "I was afraid for you. I didn't know if you made it. If you got caught." She then noticed Tunde, with the odd mixture of curiosity and hesitance peculiar to the nonparent. Picking him up, she marveled, "My God, he looks just like you." We ate lunch while Tunde slept, and over steaming cups of cocoa we talked.

"Everyone wants to know what happened and why. Even when they don't ask, I can see the question in their eyes, hear it behind every word they say."

"I'm not gonna ask you what happened," she promised. "Your letters told me a lot. I talked to my mother last night. She said that a lot of this you'll have to go through alone. And she warned me not to push you for answers and explanations."

"I don't know much about what I feel, but I know I feel bad. Leaving Femi hasn't made the pain go away."

"This pain you feel is a new pain, different, that's grown out of the old one," she said.

I stood up and walked over to the mantelpiece, where my mother's philodendrons sat, glorious and healthy. "I feel like a failure, like I'll never do anything right again. I feel guilty for the way I left. And I'm mad at having to start all over again."

"You can stay here as long as you need to—you know that—but have you any plans?"

"I'm going to Boston in a few days. Settle with a friend there. She's a woman who was an exchange student at the university for a year. We became friends. She invited me to stay with her if I needed to."

"What's in Boston?"

"Well, it's not D.C. or New York, and I think I could get a job teaching there."

"How're you fixed for money?"

"I've got fifteen hundred dollars. But it won't last long and I'll have to get some kind of job soon."

Inside Judith Prince's two-story house I licked my wounds and studied the new city I'd chosen to call home. Judith was a forty-year-old divorcée. I had noticed her sitting at the back of one of my classes one afternoon. When the class was over, she came to my desk and asked, "Are you an American?" My answer initiated a friendship as intense as it was immediately comfortable. Phoenixlike she was when we met about the business of landscaping an entirely new life. After years as a housewife, mother and active community worker volunteering for a myriad of causes, she had shifted gears. At thirty-five she divorced her husband and entered college for the first time as a full-time student. When I asked her jokingly what she wanted to be when she grew up, she shot back, "A therapist, a businesswoman, a management consultant."

"Which one?" I insisted.

"All three. I figure I've got another thirty years left. I could devote ten years to each career." Years of creative nurturing of others had honed her innate empathy. The disappointments that grew like weeds in those years and that, like weeds, she battled against had made her wise. The adventure she was making of her life imbued her with an irresistible zest and attractiveness. In between classes at the university she conducted twin love affairs with Nigerians. Both lovers gave her Nigerian names, one in Igbo and one in Yoruba. Both lavished gifts and both wanted to keep her as a prize. Her tiny dormitory room became for us a confessional and oasis as we traded impressions of Nigeria, slowly removed the gauze from our souls, the tissue paper from our dreams.

For three months Tunde and I lived in the upstairs bedroom of her house. The first few weeks she allowed me to land, to gain a semblance of emotional equilibrium. But my attempts to repair the ruptures only pushed me further into mourning and grief. Ridden with guilt, I denied that I felt any. Increasingly I turned in on myself. In this world in which I lived only the needs of my son mattered.

Finally she cracked through the fortress, accusing me, with a harshness meant to wake me from deadly slumber, of selfishness and inconsiderateness. "Maybe you wouldn't feel so bad if you did something for somebody else," she said. Her charge rallied me and I wrote a letter to my uncle and began the slow mending of fences he and I had never dared to touch. I spent a weekend with an aunt in New Bedford, fifty miles from Boston. And I began the search for a job.

I had asked Anita to pick up my mail and forward it to me. Inside one of her letters I found a note from Femi. In her letter she related how one day when she went to pick up my mail she found Femi waiting for her. She assured me she did not give him my address but said that he asked her to forward the enclosed letter to me. As I had expected, the letter was angry and obscene. A torrential outburst of confusion and frustration. While it made no threats, it left me trembling and fearful as I slipped it back into its envelope. That night Wanda called me from New York. She had received a call from one of Femi's cousins whom she dated once. He asked her if she knew where I was. The cousin explained that, according to Femi, I had apparently gone inexplicably mad and left Nigeria with Tunde. Femi, he told her, said he was afraid of what I might do to myself and our child.

During the first months in Boston it seemed to have been an inauspicious choice at best, a downright mistake at worst. I arrived at a time when a series of brutal murders plagued the city's black neighborhoods. All the victims were black women, and a sense of terror and helplessness sunk deep into my spirit. After three and a half years in Nigeria, where Black Power was a reality, I found Boston's racial climate nearly unbearable. Its small black population exerted little political influence and lacked the savvy of blacks in New York City. The citizens were divided ethnically and racially, and Boston's close-knit, insular Irish and Italian neighborhoods struck me as examples of U.S.-style tribalism.

By the end of the summer I had my own apartment and a job teaching at a junior college. But day-care costs for Tunde and the expenses of setting up house regularly depleted my salary. I was starting from scratch. Friends donated pots and pans. I hunted the thrift shops for clothes for myself and my son. And in my apartment the first two weeks I slept on the floor on a twin-size mattress with my son. I began free-lancing for a local newspaper, and Sidney Offit cheered me on as I struggled to begin writing about what I had lived through. But very few blacks were interested in my tales of Africa. They had all taken two-week trips to Ghana or Senegal and preferred their surface impressions to my intimate knowledge.

In the fall Anita forwarded another letter from Femi. The tone was conciliatory, and this time he offered me a second chance that I no longer wanted.

My dear wife:
In the months since you left, I've suffered more than you can know. I cannot, in all honesty, think of anything I could have done to earn such punishment. If I was angry with

anyone, it was with myself for the shortcomings of my busi-
ness and my failure to give you all the things I wanted to.
Without you here I find no reason to go through each day.
There has been no one else in my life since you left me.
There is no one else that I want. I miss you. I miss our son.
You will be happy to hear, I am sure, that I was recently
commissioned by Chief Jegede to design and supervise
construction of the shopping center idea I have been work-
ing on all these years. Word of this has gotten around
Lagos, and now I have more work than I can handle. Olu
Akinyemi and I have hired two assistants who will appren-
tice under me. Now I can be the husband to you that I
could not be before. All the family awaits your return.
Please come back. I will buy you anything you want to cele-
brate our reunion.

Yours faithfully,
Femi

After reading the letter, I slumped against the mailbox, my
feelings a jumble of loss, regret and anger. As I stuffed it back
into the envelope, tears that mourned the pain I had inflicted,
the pain I had endured, stung my cheeks. Mostly I cried for how
little understanding the letter revealed. I thought again of how
attuned I was to Femi's moods, how in some ways I knew him
better than myself. What, I wondered, had so utterly blinded
him to me? I believed, as his letter professed, that he loved me.
But, as I headed upstairs to my apartment, I knew that he had
never known me at all.

At night, when Tunde slept, I wrote. Lacking the energy or
desire to resurrect my novel, I turned for inspiration to the
debris of my experience. Vainly I tried to sculpt from it an object
at once sturdy and delicately wrought. This effort produced page
after page of writing. It was my story yet still a mystery to me.
The words were brittle and false. Dishonest and protective, they
informed but failed to reveal. The words were cowards that
demurred in the face of the truth. I had spun a web of words
that was choking me. Weary of fabrication, by Christmas I

stopped writing completely. I could not write because I had yet to face the backlog of passions that occupied the rooms inside the house of my memory. Those passions thrashed and knocked against the walls of that house, but propriety convinced me to hold them captive. Wanda and Judith listened to my outpourings, assuring me that one day it would all be over. But I was still unable to vent my rage, for that is what utterly consumed me behind the mask of good humor and patience I wore before the world. After months suspended in a dead zone of malaise, I began to look for a therapist. Two days before my thirtieth birthday I had my first appointment.

She was plump, with short dark brown hair and eyes that welcomed and instantly put me at ease. While she read through my folder, I scanned the faces of children and husband lining the wall behind her desk, these mementos being more prominently placed than the framed degrees. Daisies arched from the spindle-thin neck of a crystal vase on the table next to my chair. Closing the folder while sipping from a coffee mug, she asked, "What's the problem?"

We sat face to face, my hardback armchair against the wall, her swivel chair placed so that she faced me in a straight path no more than eight feet away. "I'm a writer," I began. "And I've been unable to write for several months." I looked up from my sweating hands, which were playing like impish children in my lap. "I can't write because what I'm trying to write about is too painful to remember." Her blue eyes were patient. I wondered how much complaint and angst she could bear hearing, analyzing, before she cracked.

"What are you trying to remember?"

"My marriage. My husband. Our life together." And I told her the story. Composed, pleased with the narrative I rendered, I concluded, "I feel so bad, so much anger and guilt. I've been back a year and more than anything else I hate him." My hands gathered my skirt into knots. Twisting the knots tighter, I felt myself crumbling as though an eruption had cracked the seams of once solid earth. "I hate him," I said again. And the sound of the word, finally released from its prison, hit my ears. It was fearless and liberating. I rocked back and forth in the chair, every dreaded memory hooked into me like wires. "I hate him. Oh, God, I hate him," I whispered, astonished. Sparks bounced off my words as I tallied the score. "I hate him for forcing me to tear up the life I had there. I wanted to stay. I wanted to give my son that world. But he told me he'd never let me have my child. I hate him for making me feel I had to leave like a fugitive. And I hate him most—God, I hate him—for not loving me better than he did." My hands beat my thighs as I screamed and chanted this curse. Tears overwhelmed my face until my eyes ached. And I spit out the curse, whispered and confessed it for the longest moment of my life. I damned him until I was hoarse and the tears had dried into rainbows streaking my cheeks. Spent, I sank back into the chair. "And because I hate him so," I said finally, "I can't put on paper that once I loved him."

By my third and next-to-last visit with Dr. Cassidy we had established a rapport grounded in our willingness to give each other the benefit of the doubt. This woman, who had witnessed more of my anguish and guilt than any of my family or friends, had earned my trust and respect. One afternoon, before commenting on one of my revelations, she said quietly, "Our histories are different, our experiences too. Neither of us can help that. Some of that history will confront us even as we talk. If you feel my interpretations don't adequately take into consideration all of that, tell me."

More than anything, I was locked into a sense of inadequacy because my dream of love had failed. Because love had failed me once, I was now sure it always would. "I feel so stupid. I feel as though by loving him I made a mistake that will hover over me and forever ruin every future attempt I make to love," I moaned during one session.

"Why are you so hard on yourself?" she asked in exasperation.

"To save my image of myself I deny the love I once felt. But destroying him in my mind doesn't make me feel better. It only intensifies my sense of failure."

"But you did love him," she said, leaning forward in her chair, almost reaching out to touch my still nervous hands. "And you loved him because he was a lot of the things you needed then. You've said he was confident and strong. That in the beginning, anyway, he was proud of your achievements and supportive. You loved him because these were positive things about him that you *could* love. Marita, he wasn't a monster, he was a man. You weren't an angel, you were a woman. And both of you, from what you've told me, were in love. Face up to the love," she continued. "Face up to the fact that though he hurt you, disappointed you, loving him certainly was *not* wrong. You were twenty-three years old and mourning the loss of your parents. You fell in love with him to save your life, or so you thought."

"But I gave so much. I loved him. For six years I loved the wrong man."

"When did he become the wrong man?"

"After my son was born and I started changing. Started becoming a woman I never knew lived inside me. Then I needed a man he could never be."

"But for all the time before?"

"He . . . he was what I needed," I conceded, amazed at the revelation she had produced. "So I don't have to write off that love, I don't have to destroy any memory of it?"

"No, and you couldn't even if you really wanted to. Life is a package of experience and emotions. Stop trying to force it to be only one thing, either love or hate. It's usually a little bit of both."

"And where do I go from here?"

"I have no answers, Marita. You have them. You just have to dig to get at them. You have a tremendous amount of strength. I know it doesn't feel like it at this moment. But you wouldn't be hurting so bad now if you hadn't given so much to your past. Now you've got to see just what you're going to give to your future."

Now I belonged to me. No parents or husband claiming me as alter ego or reflection. There was only my child who consumed and replenished me. Our union was as old as the universe and new every day. My son's love was unconditional and, as such, gave me more freedom than any love I had known. But how does one "become" a mother?

Nobody to teach me. Must pay for all mistakes. Discovering

my child as burden and treasure. His needs—insistent, undenia-
ble—distracted me from the farthest reaches of despair. His smile
patrolled the border leading to madness. Would not let me cross.
His presence—missed, felt—imprinted everything I was becoming. I shepherded him through toilet training, first words, temper
tantrums, discipline that was sometimes too much too little too
late. I read the books, then tossed them aside and relied on in-
stinct and the advice of other mamas. And I witnessed the growing that never stopped—minuscule and mighty. Each moment of
every day. At night, saying prayers. God bless mama, God bless
—yes—God bless daddy too. His face said it all. In sleep or repose it was me—laughing, eating energetically—and it was Femi.
My/our life, so interconnected with, dependent on, others—
baby-sitters, day-care centers, pediatricians and playmates. His
new shoes won out over a new dress for me. And I at last accepted mama as my name. Realized it did not melt down any
other designations. Discovered that it expanded them—and me—
in a cosmic way, rooted in love. But what would I do with me? I
had abruptly snatched my life out of Femi's hold. But now that
it lay in my own trembling palms, I hardly knew how to begin
shaping a new design. Slipping into old patterns, I wandered in
and out of a series of intense, unfulfilling affairs. Loving someone
else was easy. Always had been. Loving and trusting myself was
the dare yet to be accepted.

Norman, just divorced from a mate who, thanks to his talent
for dependency, had been more mother than wife, sought to
thrust the same role on me. Instead of flowers he brought me
guilt at his separation from his three sons; need, in the form of
requests for cash (his funds were depleted by alimony pay-
ments, he said); and a desire to move in with me so I could
"take care" of him and "straighten up" his life. We were tem-
peramentally incompatible, and for over a year I could neither
break off nor make peace with him. His sexual prowess and my
determination to make a relationship succeed at any cost bound
me to him. Next was Carl, an up-and-coming lawyer who swept
through my life like a brushfire in three whirlwind months.
Lacking the skills and desire to carry an affair through the long
haul, he was a flashing meteor who arrived as though he

belonged nowhere else. But when the mating dance concluded, and making what we had work out intruded its mundane demands, he fled with indecent haste.

Finally, I embarked on a period of celibacy for fourteen months. The prescription was extreme, but for what was ailing me, it was the proper cure.

These relationships had left me drained, depressed and as physically exhausted as I was emotionally. Both Carl and Norman, I reasoned while involved with them, had made me happy simply because I was not alone. But Carl's departure invoked in me a new and unfamiliar sense of relief, as though I had been relieved of a burden or stripped of chains.

I did not wake up one morning, however, and "decide" to become celibate. The decision was thrust upon me more by circumstance than plan. Initially buoyed by my breakup, I used the time immediately following it, as I generally did, to recoup, puzzle over what went wrong and wonder who my next lover would be. But as the months passed, I met few suitable men. And in the beginning I suffered what can only be termed withdrawal symptoms. To my surprise, however, the post-love affair malaise, which usually lingered until I found a new mate, this time lifted on its own. Unlike the past, the longer I was alone this time, the less fearful I became of being alone. My choice to be celibate was not saying "no" to men as much as it was saying "yes" to me. The struggle to reestablish a career and friendships, the demands of single parenthood and financial burdens turned my existence, I felt, into a quagmire some days. I wanted to be alone. More than anything, I needed to clear out the cobwebs growing like weeds in my mind.

Sexual desire did not magically disappear. There were men, even then, who could have quelled my lust, but I began to feel that to return to them was a signal of defeat. Out of pride and a blossoming self-confidence, I preferred, this time, to be alone.

By the sixth month of this adventure, which was now more about my head than my sex organs, I told Julia that I was not only celibate but was finding it a productive experience. When I told her she quipped, "I've always preferred quality to quantity. When you're by yourself you discover a stranger in your house you didn't really know—yourself. When you meet the intruder, what you find out may shock or disappoint you. But it usually makes you stronger."

My relationships with men improved. Though by the eighth month celibacy was not just a situation I was bearing but rather a choice, I still dated occasionally. There was John, with whom I shared a passion for good movies and books. Although we both experienced a fleeting, initial sexual attraction, we chose not to act on it. He, because he was in analysis and could not handle the responsibilities of a relationship. I, because I needed more time to discover the stranger Julia had told me about. If past experience was any clue, I could not do that very well while I was emotionally involved.

With Louis I shared the progress of my book and his efforts to write one of his own. Both these men taught me that I could be friends with men. Both were as supportive as my female companions—and, in time, as valued. Freed from the shackles of sexual expectation, I discovered the compassion, humor and wisdom in men that I had been blinded to before. For the first time I did not feel slighted when a man I cared for failed to make a pass. Both John and Louis enjoyed my company and respected my views. The absence of sexual desire merely confirmed that there was more to me, and to them, than sex. My frame of mind had liberated us from the sexual prison in which I had served so much time. In the past I had endowed sex with the ability to provide happiness and banish loneliness. Sex, I was certain, made everything alright. But celibacy helped me to put sex in perspective. It taught me the difference between honest sexual desire and mere sexual need.

That year was the most fertile period I'd known. Buoyed by energies I'd released in the past through sex, my writing was a steady eruption. I savored the day-by-day growth of my son. Made new friends and pampered the old ones. I came to trust my own judgments and instincts.

But, most of all, this was a time to think about me. I reviewed and analyzed my past in the quiet hours after Tunde had gone to sleep, asking the hard questions I had shrunk from before, fashioning honest answers that gave me strength. This emotional as well as sexual fast informed me that after years of gorging myself on romantic illusions of love, I hardly knew the real thing. Always I had looked to men to tell me who I was. Now I was willing and able to provide my own answers.

I knew myself better. Liked myself more. I had discovered not just how to say "no" but when to. Womanhood was a process, not a destination. I had crawled. Now I was standing. I could not wait to take the first step.

24

One weekend I visited Wanda. Our friendship at every moment of its life had always been what I needed. Resilient, fragile, expansive and stubborn, it continued to amaze and serve us. In my absence she had become a woman of keener, larger spirit. She clung less and reached more. Her friendship flattered and redeemed me. Experience had fingerprinted us differently. Yet our vision of ourselves was the same. And was reflected in each other's eyes.

Washington Square Park swirled with colors and people that Saturday afternoon in the spring. We watched Tunde playing in a sandbox not far from the bench where we sat.

"I wrote Femi," I told her.

"You've written him before. Did you mail the letter this time?"

"Yes."

Surprised, she looked at me closely. "What did you say?"

"Everything. Mostly that we can't go back to what we had. That it's over. That I want a divorce."

"Was it hard to write the letter?"

"Yes. It was even harder to mail it."

"You look good," she said slowly, appraising me openly. "You sound good too. Better than before."

"Anything's better than before." I shrugged.

"You know what I mean."

"I guess I do. It's amazing how difficult loving can be." I reflected. "How easy it is to love Tunde. How impossible it was to love Femi in the end."

Suddenly smiling bravely, she said, "How wonderful it was to love Femi at the start."

"That love saved me, I know that now." I conceded. "That's why I couldn't let it turn on me. I couldn't let it destroy us."

"The only thing I'm gonna say, kid, is you're gonna be alright."

"Nothing more profound or earth-shattering than that?" I asked, feigning disappointment.

"Nope, just you're gonna be alright."

I hugged her and closed my eyes. Resting my head on her narrow shoulder, I said a fast silent prayer of thanks for everything I had lived through and known. Opening my eyes, the sun shone into the pools of joy forming there. For, after a season of fitful migration, I had come home. To rest against the bedrock inside myself. I had wandered. Will wander still . . . and will take home with me wherever I go.